Feeling the Spirit

STUDIES IN COMPARATIVE RELIGION

Frederick M. Denny, General Editor

FEELING THE SPIRIT

Faith and Hope
in an Evangelical
Black Storefront Church

Frances Kostarelos

University of South Carolina Press

Published in Columbia, South Carolina, by the
University of South Carolina Press

Manufactured in the United States of America

99 98 97 96 95   5 4 3 2 1

Library of Congress Cataloging-in-Publication Data

Kostarelos, Frances, 1956–
    Feeling the spirit : faith and hope in an evangelical Black
storefront church/Frances Kostarelos.
        p. cm. — (Studies in comparative religion)
    Includes bibliographical references and index.
    ISBN 1–57003–051–0
    1. Afro–American Baptists—Illinois—Chicago—History—20th
century. 2. Chicago (Ill.)—Church History—20th century.
I. Title. II. Series: Studies in comparative religion (Columbia,
S.C.)
BX6445.C4K67 1995
286'.177311—dc20   95-4336
                                                    CIP

For Abishi and Theodora

CONTENTS

ILLUSTRATIONS

GENERAL EDITOR'S PREFACE

Since its inception in the nineteenth century, the academic study of religion—whether under the name comparative religion, history of religions, anthropology of religion—has mostly concerned either non-western world religions, ancient religions with surviving texts, or the religions of tribal, small-scale cultures that have usually been exclusively oral. Christianity has generally been the domain of seminary-grounded fields such as theology, church history, biblical studies, and liturgics.

Frances Kostarelos's historical ethnography of an evangelical black storefront church on Chicago's West Side is a refreshing addition to the literature on both Christianity and religion in the United States. The ethnographic approach takes one into what for most readers is a largely unknown, even remote world of black working-class religious poor in the urban North. The seasoned reader of traditional religious ethnography expects to learn about the cosmologies, myths, and rituals of the likes of Inuit, Dinka, Melanesian, or Bororo people. But the reader of studies about western Christian societies is unaccustomed to learning about the "cosmology" of an urban congregation and how it is "structured by . . . a symbolic rendering of the life, teachings, death, and resurrection of Jesus, who in their collective thought is the son of God and the savior of humanity." Kostarelos shows how this vision is not simply a theological discourse but a lived reality among the members of First Corinthians M.B.C.

Kostarelos is a practitioner of the new ethnography, whereby people studied also participate in reviewing and validating what is being written about them. This is participant-observation in a truly inclusive sense, with texts that "talk back." In the process of describing and interpreting the history, organization, beliefs, worship practices, and other activities of the church, Kostarelos reveals a great deal about the hurts, hopes, struggles, and triumphs of this kind of Christian community. Her theoretical perspective effectively draws on both Durkheim's conception of religion as a "sacred collective consciousness" and Weber's concept of charismatic authority. Kostarelos portrays a way of inner-city urban life in which people are still striving to shape their identity as black people and to take collective action in a period when increasing inner-city poverty and the breakdown of institutions appear to be overwhelming obstacles.

Frederick Mathewson Denny

PREFACE

The principal settings for my research for this book were First Corinthians Missionary Baptist Church (a fictitious name, which I will sometimes abbreviate as First Corinthians M.B.C.) and the homes of members of its congregation, located in predominantly black low-income neighborhoods on the West Side of Chicago. Through observation as a participant in the church, by taking part in the day-to-day activities of several households, and through in-depth interviews with church leaders and other members, I sought to understand the religious cosmos of church members and the role of their sacred vision in constructing their social world. My research was conducted from 1983 to 1986. While in the field, I made lasting friendships with members of First Corinthians M.B.C. Through my experiences with them I gained a deeper understanding of their religious conceptions and their everyday life.

Like other anthropologists who have worked among working-class and impoverished blacks in the urban North in the United States (Liebow 1967; Hannerz 1969; Stack 1974; Aschenbrenner 1975; Anderson 1978; Rose 1987), I became part of a group and of everyday social action in a black ghetto through people who live there. I met two sisters, Jackie Evans and Annie Larson (their names too are fictitious, as are the names of all church members in this account), who are members of First Corinthians M.B.C. while I was working in a medical clinic less than three miles from their church. When I met Jackie, she was twenty-nine years old, was married to Joseph Evans, and had two daughters. Joseph and Jackie Evans owned their home, a two-story building on the West Side. Joseph is a foreman in a suburban chemical factory, and Jackie is a housewife. At the time I met Annie Larson, she had never been married;

she had two children. She was dating James Davis, who was the father of the child she was carrying when I met her at the clinic. Annie was on welfare. James worked at the chemical factory with Joseph Evans and helped Annie support herself and the children.

I came to know Jackie and Annie better during the summer of 1981 while interviewing them in Jackie's house—where Annie was then living with her children—for a study I was conducting on infant feeding practices among low-income black women. This was one of twelve households I visited regularly that summer. I first went to Jackie's house on a weekday morning; she and Annie were in the midst of doing laundry, housecleaning, and cooking and caring for the children. Annie offered me a cup of coffee, and we talked while they carried out their chores. Annie especially liked to talk about daily household chores, child care, and cooking. She explained that she practiced the "old ways" she had learned from "mama and them." From her mother, Linda Larson, she had learned to value a clean home, clean clothes, and home cooking. Annie said, "When I was young, you could eat off that floor in mama's house. There wasn't a speck of dust on the wood. When it came to chores, mama would get me and Jackie if we didn't do what she said do."

My visit with Jackie Evans and Annie Larson lasted the entire day. Toward the early evening, Jackie said that they had to get ready to go to church to rehearse for the Gospel Choir anniversary, which was to take place on Sunday. We had spent most of the day talking about household matters and life in the neighborhood; this was the first I had heard about their church. Jackie explained its importance by saying, "Church is where me and my family stay most of the time, and you need to come there if you want to know about us." At the end of our visit, they invited me to First Corinthians M.B.C. for the Gospel Choir anniversary that Sunday.

I went to First Corinthians M.B.C. on Sunday. Annie was standing outside the church when I arrived and was pleased to see me. During the program I sat with Annie Larson and Jackie's children. Jackie is a soloist and was performing that evening. Before she sang, she introduced me to the congregation as her doctor's secretary. She welcomed me to the church and expressed the hope that I would enjoy myself and find inspiration in the evening's program. After the performance Jackie and Annie introduced me to their family and friends. That evening I met their pastor, Rev. James Thomas, and other church members, including Deacon B. J. Clark, Rev. Frank Dixon, Rev. Allen Tyson, and Rev. Tyson's wife, Josephine Tyson. Just before I left the fellowship hall, Rev. Tyson said, "We're sure glad to have you. Come back to the House of the Lord and fellowship with us anytime."

I continued to see Jackie Evans and Annie Larson at the clinic; they were both pregnant that year and came there for routine prenatal care. We talked about the church and the people I had met there. They enthusiastically informed me of future services and said I should visit again. As Jackie put it, "There is always something worth going to at church; every day of the week there is something to do." Over the next two years I periodically attended worship services and other programs at First Corinthians M.B.C. During those two years Jackie and Annie invited me to their homes for dinners, card games, birthdays, and anniversaries (Annie moved to an apartment across the street from Jackie's house in 1983 with James Davis and her children). Most of the people who came to these affairs were relatives and friends from First Corinthians M.B.C., and thus I gradually came to know a wider circle of people from the congregation.

In 1983 Rev. James Thomas gave me permission to conduct field research in the church. From September of that year until December 1985 I was intensively involved in the day-to-day activities of First Corinthians M.B.C. I was allowed to tape worship services and interviews with church members. I interviewed Rev. Thomas several times in his office, which gave me an opportunity to discuss his calling, the history of the church, and the people who had founded the church and developed its programs. Assistant ministers, deacons, and other officers also were generous with their time and patiently answered my questions.

Annie Larson and Jackie Evans introduced me to Angela and Don Williams, who became my friends and significant guides at First Corinthians M.B.C. While I had seen this couple at church many times, I did not get to know them personally until I ran into Angela Williams in a clothing shop near the church where she had started to work a month earlier. That day she looked tired and said she could hardly stand on her feet because she felt dizzy and weak. I suggested that she see a doctor if she did not feel better. Two weeks later she came to the clinic with Annie Larson. For the next few months she came to the clinic regularly, and we became friends. Over the years, my friendship with Angela and Don helped me to understand the relationship between their religious ideas and practices and their family life. In May 1983 I attended their fourteenth wedding anniversary celebration given by their "church family" at the Nimbus Disco.

Angela Williams was in her early thirties when we met. She was the teacher for the Junior Women's Mission Circle Bible class, which she invited me to join. As a member of her class I attended midweek prayer and healing services and Bible class. In the class I listened to women interpret their experiences in the light of Scripture; I had the same opportunity in Sunday school, which included men. As a participant in these church Bible study groups, I gained a better understanding of the spiritual principles articulated at First Corinthians M.B.C. as its members use them to make sense of everyday life.

As a member of the Mission Circle I also went to worship services and programs held in other evangelical storefront churches in Chicago. Members of First Corinthians M.B.C. often visit other storefront congregations for anniversaries, baptisms, funerals, weddings, and gospel music recitals. They also make trips to sing and worship in what they consider their home churches in the South throughout the year, and all church members are welcome to go on them. I went to Mississippi and Alabama in August 1984 with a church group that has been going on this trip annually since 1972. On these trips my role was to baby-sit small children while their parents performed.

Throughout my first year at First Corinthians M.B.C. I was known as Jackie Evans and Annie Larson's "doctor's secretary who wanted to know something about the church." When I joined the Junior Women's Mission Circle, church members started to call me Sister Fran. After my first year of attendance at First Corinthians, a senior woman said to me, "Francine, you should just go ahead and join this church and get right in there with us." Others also suggested that since I was spending so much time with them, the only thing to do was to join. I explained that I was Greek Orthodox, that I was a graduate anthropology student, and that I was gathering information to write about First Corinthians M.B.C. Although I did not formally join First Corinthians M.B.C., when I visit there, Rev. James Thomas introduces me to the congregation as a friend and member of the church.

In the autumn of 1986 I gave a copy of the chapters I had completed to Rev. Thomas and another to Angela Williams. He read and approved the work. His only critical comment was about my use of fictitious names; he questioned why I did not use his real name and the real name of the church. Angela arranged a dinner party in her home and invited our Bible study group to read my work. That evening the group took turns reading parts of it to each other. Before we left her house, Rev. Arthur

Johnson offered a prayer thanking God for blessing me with the Spirit to stay among them to write about the church. He also prayed for my strength to finish the book. Angela offered a prayer and shared her vision of my work with the group: "Now, you know God works in mysterious ways. To find Sister Fran and bring her from the big white university to this big black church on the West Side, that's something. God knew nobody in our church had the education to do what he wanted her to do. God knew we needed someone to help us get the word out, and that's why he put the Spirit in her and blessed her to fellowship with us."

According to my church friends and Bible study group, God gives everyone he sends to First Corinthians M.B.C. a job to do there and the ability to get it done through a special gift, known as charisma. The importance of charisma at First Corinthians M.B.C. was made clear to me when I asked Angela to suggest a fictitious name for the church. She suggested the name First Corinthians Missionary Baptist Church because the congregation reminded her of the Corinthians Saint Paul addressed in his letters. She explained that, like the Corinthians, members of her church had God-given gifts—love, faith, charity, and wisdom—to use in running the church. In her view, love is the most important gift. Without love, she explained, there are envy and conflict, which undermine unity and Christian spirit.

Over the years the church members explained my presence and field work in their church according to their way of thinking. From their perspective, a young white women devoting herself to a black church in a run-down and dangerous neighborhood was the work of God. God wanted me to see what the church was about for my salvation and for the spiritual enlightenment of others who would read my work. As Rev. Thomas puts it, through "the mingling and commingling" of our voices in Bible study, worship services, prayer meetings, and Missionary Circle rounds, my friends showed me that their faith, humility, patience, love, and kindness provide dignity and courage in the face of personal setbacks, social injustice, suffering, and uncertainty.

Since 1986 I have returned to First Corinthians M.B.C. for the celebration of the pastor's anniversary, the church anniversary, the Heavenly Knights' anniversary, and the Larson Singers' anniversary. In 1986 Don and Angela Williams asked me to be their daughter Sante Anna's godmother. Church friends call and invite me to attend baptisms, weddings, funerals, and fund-raising programs. They also invite me to their homes for holidays, birthdays, anniversaries, card games, and dinners as they did before.

My successful field work on the West Side of Chicago was made possible by church cosmology, which welcomes the stranger, and by the presence of several articulate men and women in the church who were willing to teach me about their beliefs and practices. I also had the good fortune to arrive at First Corinthians M.B.C. at a time when the congregation was stable under the leadership of James Thomas. It was his decision to allow me to work there, and his authority assured that I would get the cooperation I needed from the congregation.

There are others to whom I owe thanks. At the University of Chicago I was privileged to work with professors Ralph Nicholas, Jean Comaroff, William Julius Wilson, Raymond Fogelson, Sol Tax, Richard Chrisman, and Renee Valeri. I am grateful to them for helping me develop the ideas that influenced this book.

I thank the late Professor Romney Moseley for reading an earlier draft of the work and for his belief that oppressed Christians have a great deal to teach us about God and humanity, which sustained my work in difficult moments.

Thanks to Marta Nicholas, Howard Miller, Angela Perez, Peter Grabas, Maria Gebhard, Rev. Mary T. Carr, William Kaufman, Rosemary Camilleri, and Bonita Street for moral support and friendship. I thank Arturo Giraldez, Anthony Barrett, Esmerlda Medina, Richard Sakurai, Sandy Sakurai, Katie Golsan, Susan Giraldez, and Christine Schnusenburg for enjoyable and informative conversations about religious symbols and human practice.

For funds to conduct field research I am grateful to the University of Chicago's Department of Anthropology. I thank the Institute for the Study of American Evangelicals, Wheaton College, for support that enabled me to write early drafts of this work and for the opportunity to present parts of it to other scholars who provided invaluable and perceptive advice.

I thank my husband, Abishi, and our daughter, Theodora, for their love and patience.

But my greatest debt is to the First Corinthians Missionary Baptist Church congregation for years of generous hospitality and assistance, which have made this book possible.

Feeling the Spirit

INTRODUCTION

Evangelical storefront churches are pervasive in black working-class and poverty-stricken neighborhoods in the urban North. This book is about the cosmology and practices articulated in a storefront congregation. The interpretation is guided by cultural anthropological study of religious beliefs and practices as they relate to the construction of collective consciousness, social solidarity, and resistance to social and economic oppression among racial, economic, and political minorities. The locus of the study is First Corinthians Missionary Baptist Church (a fictitious name, as I have explained in the preface), a storefront church founded in 1950 on the West Side of Chicago by a small group of black evangelicals who had migrated from the South in the late 1940s.

My purpose is to elucidate through historical and ethnographic analysis the symbols and meanings encoded in the collective thought and practices of the congregation, to explicate the church's conception of God and its vision of God's grace in human affairs and in the cosmos. In so doing, I argue that First Corinthians M.B.C. is structured by the congregation's symbolic rendering of the life, teachings, death, and resurrection of Jesus, who in their collective thought is the son of God and the savior of humanity. I will show that in the context of church routines, the congregation articulates narratives based on its interpretation of Scripture to give meaning to its members' lives and to create moral and social solidarity in the midst of the hardships of the ghetto. I will also demonstrate that the collective principles articulated at First Corinthians M.B.C. resist and reverse degrading images of blacks that are the consequence of uneven economic distribution and race discrimination. The moral and social teachings of the church posit a vision of black spiritual qualities and identity that oppose white contempt and demeaning dispositions toward impoverished inner-city blacks. Throughout this analysis it is apparent that individual and group activity in this church is informed by the congregation's vision of God's distribution of spiritual gifts (charisma) among them.

The argument that black evangelical religion constitutes an empassioned response to racial oppression and black economic subordination contrasts with existing sociological and anthropological interpretations (Sutherland 1928; Daniel 1940, 1942; Drake 1940; Drake and Cayton 1945; Eddy 1958; Harrison 1966; Fauset 1971; Williams 1974; Paris 1982). These analysts view storefront churches as ephemeral ghetto locales defined by otherworldly and compensatory beliefs and practices that help poor blacks adapt to social and economic hardship and injustice. They assume before systematic empirical investigation that religious thought and practice are a consequence of ghetto pathology. In their schema, religion functions to ease anxiety and frustration. The existing literature is guided by social theory that overlooked the history of the black church and black theology and thus missed the potential that working-class black religion embodies for helping its adherents construct a usable past, social values, and collective purpose.

Contrary to existing studies, which view the storefront church as black accommodation and capitulation to white power, my account argues that within these churches, black evangelicals define a worldview that withstands the self-interested principles defined in the American mainstream. In my interpretation, evangelical storefront churches are considered a part of the three-hundred-year legacy of black struggle against white oppression and racism in America, and the narratives and practices at First Corinthians M.B.C. replace disparaging images of inner-city blacks with a meaningful vision of collective black suffering, hope, and self-determination.

The Theory:
Charismatic Authority in the Storefront Congregation

My interpretation has drawn from Durkheim's (1965) conception of religion as sacred collective consciousness, Weber's (1978:399–634) study of charismatic authority in religious movements among the urban poor, and anthropologists who have studied religious representations among oppressed evangelical Protestants in the Third World. I am guided by Durkheim's argument that the study of religion is concerned with sacred conceptual categories and the relationship between the principles encoded in them and the construction of collective moral and social order and solidarity. In his schema, a church is constituted by a group that is united by a shared system of sacred beliefs and practices. He argued that the system of beliefs and practices embodied in a church are also a source of moral and social solidarity (1965:59). Following Durkheim, this book discusses the system of shared sacred conceptions as they shape the development of spiritual leadership in the congregation, the constitution of the church organization, and the construction of routine church activities.

Like Durkheim, Weber argued that religion constitutes a conceptual system that meaningfully defines and orders the world for a group that adheres to the principles embedded in that system. In my discussion of the development of church organization and spiritual vocations I am guided by Weber's conception of the charismatic prophet and the routinization of charismatic authority. Weber argued that a prophet is a religious leader who claims authority on the basis of a charismatic endowment—unlike a priest, who depends on formal training in a sacred tradition. According to Weber, a prophet believes he or she has a God-given calling and spiritual gifts to lead a mission. In Weber's schema, a prophet's gifts include the ability to receive divine revelations and to mediate God's word and grace for humanity. The prophet's words and deeds encode symbols that meaningfully order the world and the place of human beings in that world. Weber suggested that the purpose of the charismatic prophet's mission is to teach human beings God's plan for their salvation (1978:450–451).

Religious authority in black evangelical thought is based on a vision of spiritual gifts evident in the voice, ideas, bearing, and action of individuals and groups. Weber argued that a group that recognizes the extraordinary spiritual gifts of an individual seeks to make those gifts permanent by establishing institutions in which they routinely invest their time, labor, and resources. He held that groups that create and participate in institutions based on charismatic authority share the social, moral, and spiritual principles articulated by their leader. I will elucidate the principles that structure the routines of the congregation and discuss the collective assumptions that predispose church members to work and give their resources to the church. It is apparent that their actions in church are informed by their understanding of God's moral and social rules for humanity's salvation.

There are countless evangelical storefront churches on main streets in black ghettos where poverty and the disfiguring marks of socioeconomic injustice and racism abound. Individuals who belong to these storefront churches daily confront the harsh exigencies of ghetto living—joblessness, inadequate social welfare programs, poverty, and racism. At the beginning of this introduction I indicated that my analysis departs from the analyses of sociologists and anthropologists who have suggested that black storefront religion is a capitulation and accommodation to white economic and social power. My study concurs with Comaroff's (1985) and Lancaster's (1988) arguments that evangelical Protestant discourse and practice among oppressed racial, economic, and political minorities in the Third World constitute a counterhegemonic discourse. These writers have shown that impoverished evangelical Protestants redefine the cosmos according to their biblical vision of divine authority over human and cosmic affairs. In their analyses, economically and socially oppressed evangelicals create in their collective religious imagination, discourse, and practice spiritual symbols and principles that displace the oppressive symbols of powerful groups and critique an economic system that provides wealth for a few while leaving the masses in poverty.

Thus, throughout the following chapters, my aim is to elaborate the symbols and meanings encoded in the collective thought of members of First Corinthians M.B.C. The ethnographic chapters of this book are preceded by a discussion of the ideas black evangelicals articulated in the 1700s and 1800s. The purpose of the historical perspective I have taken is to show that the black evangelical cosmos created in black ghettos of the urban North are a continuation of a three-hundred-year history of meaningful black evangelical discourse and practice. This account suggests that the symbols embodied in black evangelical thought have been a source of ideas and action for resisting oppression, racial discrimination, and socioeconomic injustice. My analysis refutes the argument that black religion is otherworldly and a result of the pathologies of ghetto living. It suggests that the symbolic categories defined in the black storefront church are a source of ideas and practices for black self-determination in the face of white discrimination, economic underdevelopment, and social disorganization.

Summary of Chapters

Chapter one centers on the development of black evangelical thought and independent black churches in the eighteenth and nineteenth centuries under slavery. The purpose of this discussion is to consider ideas and social processes that gave way to the expansion of evangelical storefront churches in American cities. I will show that blacks converted in great numbers because they saw in evangelical Protestant thought spiritual principles that delivered them from bondage and social injustice. The chapter also considers the growth of the black church in Chicago in the 1900s. It focuses on the influence of race and class discrimination on black institutions during the period of migration and urbanization and on the place of the black church in resistance to white oppression and socioeconomic subordination among the black masses.

Economic underdevelopment among urban blacks in the 1980s and concomitant social problems are the subjects of chapter two. This discussion primarily considers the predominantly poor and black areas on the West Side of Chicago, where First Corinthians M.B.C. is located and where most of the members of this congregation live. My aim in this chapter is to discuss the everyday exigencies in the black inner city that have resulted from a failed economy and racial discrimination. This chapter describes day-to-day experiences that, in my view, inform the narration and interpretation of the biblical story at First Corinthians M.B.C.

In the third chapter, I discuss the founding of First Corinthians M.B.C, considering first the life and ideas of Rev. James Thomas, who was called to lead First Corinthians in the mid-1960s. The discussion is based on his account of his early years in the South and the events of the 1940s and 1950s that led to his calling. I also discuss life histories of individuals who helped define principles and create programs that constitute First Corinthians M.B.C. I focus on the place of belief in divine agency and spiritual gifts in making evangelical storefront missions and spiritual vocations.

Chapter four elucidates principles embedded in First Corinthians M.B.C. cosmology. It contains a discussion of the congregation's vision of God in human affairs and in the cosmos and an examination of the principles that determine the organizational structure of First Corinthians M.B.C. I consider the volunteer jobs members do on church committees, boards, and offices with a focus on the spiritual principles that underlie the making of church vocations and the congregation's perspective on the meaning and purpose of human labor. It is apparent that church principles give meaning to the labor members perform in the church and in the blue-collar workplaces where most of them earn or seek to earn their living. I also show that storefront church careers are a source of personal meaning, status, and recognition for low-income blacks who lack resources and skills to compete for prestigious work in the American mainstream. In the last two sections I discuss the collective spiritual principles underlying church finances and the collective ideas and objectives guiding the construction of space used for worship and community programs.

Chapter five provides a discussion of the system of shared sacred ideas represented in worship services, Bible study, and prayer meetings at First Corinthians M.B.C. The primary focus is on activities held on the first Sunday of every month, which, according to the congregation's members, is the most active and spiritually significant day of the month. In the final section of this chapter I focus on the major midweek events. My aim here is to further explicate the congregation's vision of God's agency in everyday human transactions. I will show that through their collective interpretation of the Christian story created and recreated in church practices, congregants meaningfully order their everyday experiences.

Black families living in the impoverished inner city have been the subject of academic and public controversy over the past twenty-five years. Much of the discussion, however, overlooks the place of religion in structuring family and household organization. The intent of chapter six is to shed light on the relationship between church participation among working-class blacks and their family identity and solidarity. This chapter considers the history of the extended family of Angela and Don Williams and the spiritual principles they and other church members follow to stem the fragmentation of family life resulting from the decline of blue-collar industry, on which they have depended since they settled in Chicago in the late 1950s.

The concluding chapter provides a summary of the main arguments of the book and reflects on the future of the evangelical storefront congregation in shaping black identity and collective action in the face of greater inner-city economic decline and increasing institutional dislocation and social tension.

CHAPTER ONE

The Historical and Social Context

Charisma and Black Liberation

Blacks in the South were converted to Christianity in the late 1700s and early 1800s by white evangelical Protestants who believed that God's love, mercy, and gift of salvation through faith in Jesus were for all of humanity (Mathews 1977:69–70). While some reform-minded white evangelicals believed in God-given freedom and grace for all humanity and worked to end slavery, others opposed them as they feared and resented black spiritual equality and freedom (Genovese 1974:183–209; Raboteau 1978:96–128, 143–45). White opposition, however, did not prevent blacks from converting to Christianity and struggling for liberation. Blacks who accepted Christianity believed that they were obligated to challenge institutions and practices that violated the will of a merciful and loving God. Blacks became Christians in massive numbers when they saw in evangelical Protestantism a cosmological order that gave meaning to their suffering and delivered them from bondage (Genovese 1974:163–65; Mathews 1977:66–68; Raboteau 1978:212–19; West 1982:15–20). In the Scripture, black evangelicals saw a powerful God who intervened in human and worldly affairs to vindicate the poor and to liberate oppressed people. In evangelical conception, God was an eternal ruler in heaven, where faith in Jesus would deliver them. They envisioned a God who ruled over their ephemeral and evil masters on earth. Black evangelicals believed that God knew about their suffering and would deliver mercy, justice, and liberation to them as He had to other enslaved biblical peoples. In evangelicalism blacks found a God they could talk to personally at all times without the mediation of the clergy. In the evangelical cosmos, all human beings are created equal in the eyes of God, and blacks were drawn by the egalitarian principles embedded in evangelical thought.

Throughout the antebellum period, whites who feared and despised black Christians aimed to control black religious thought and experience. On plantations, white patrols sought to prevent slaves from gathering for worship. In churches whites demeaned blacks by forcing them to sit apart. In white-controlled churches, blacks could not serve in church offices and had no voice in church affairs. Slave owners demanded that both black and white preachers use Scripture and worship services to instruct slaves to obey their masters and to accept their subservient position. White attempts to use evangelical religion as a means of social control, however, failed as enslaved Christians contested slavery and the denial of spiritual rights. In the evangelical world, individual salvation is contingent on the will of God, which human beings can not mediate. In black evangelical thought, white supremacy is dismantled by God's will and dispensations that rule over human destiny. Black interpretation of biblical narratives gave them the authority to challenge white racist claims and to reject instruction and preaching that praised white power over black (Raboteau 1978:290–318; Genovese 1974:232–55).

The black vision of God as a personal, just, and merciful savior of humble and oppressed people mobilized resistance against slavery and white supremacy. Black spiritual beliefs embodied a providential promise of equality and freedom. Black consciousness defied white racist intransigence. Blacks rejected the degrading and subservient position whites imposed on them in church. To fulfill their covenant with God, enslaved blacks gathered secretly in the brush and river banks to worship, free from white control and circumspection. In these "invisible" churches blacks worshipped God on their own terms and articulated religious principles that elevated their status (Genovese 1974:255–79; Raboteau 1978:212–19). Away from white supervision, black men and women cultivated what they perceived to be their God-given gifts of faith, wisdom, and prophecy. They were led by people from their own ranks who depended on God to define and guide their mission.

The invisible plantation churches, structured by the religious imagination of enslaved black men and women, harbored the beginnings of black autonomy and self-determination (Raboteau 1978:212–19). The invisible church gave way to separate and independent black churches. The establishment of independent black churches in the late 1700s and early 1800s is considered the first black freedom movement (Wilmore 1983:78–98); their creation represented a massive black rejection of segregation. Within them blacks mobilized collective efforts to undermine white supremacy and dismantle slavery (Wilmore 1983:78–98).

Throughout the 1800s, spiritually gifted black leaders led the movement to resist white over black authority. Among some of the better-known black religious pioneers are Absolom Jones, Richard Allen, Andrew Bryan, James Varrick, and Morris Brown; in the name of a liberating God, they and other black leaders led blacks out of demeaning and oppressive white churches and mobilized black spiritual and material support for independent black churches (Wilmore 1983:78–98). Although they were at times brutally beaten and intimidated by whites, they remained true to their faith in a liberating God and did not abandon the movement for black self-determination; white brutality and the threat of violence only strengthened black Christians to resist oppression. The slave insurrections led by Gabriel Prosser in 1800, Denmark Vesey in 1822, and Nat Turner in 1831 were inspired by their leaders' religious convictions. These men and their followers studied the Bible and had faith in a merciful and liberating God. Gabriel, Vesey, and Turner identified with and emulated the Old Testament prophets who led their people out of bondage (Wilmore 1983:53–73).

In the years following the Civil War, white Southerners continued to assert the doctrine of white supremacy and used the legal and state apparatus to deny blacks political, economic, and civil rights. After emancipation, the struggle for black social and economic justice was sustained in black religious vision and supported by independent black churches (Wilmore 1983:135–66; Morris 1984:4–12). In their churches blacks achieved autonomy and control over their lives at a time when white oppression was unrelenting. In their separate churches, before and after emancipation, blacks defined and pursued spiritual, social, cultural, and political interests. From the inception of the black church, the mission included a collective commitment to unencumbered worship, black self-determination, and social welfare (Wilmore 1983:74–98). Black churches developed social programs to oppose white restrictions against black equality and participation. For example, whites denied blacks political power by ruling that only literate black men could vote. For the masses of black freedmen, adults and children, the church Sunday school provided the only opportunity to learn to read and write. While the white Sunday schools of the late 1800s were dedicated to teaching Christian principles and discipline, blacks sought self-improvement and political empowerment by learning to read and write in their Sunday schools (Woodson 1921; Boylan 1988). The Sunday school and other programs blacks developed in their independent churches in the late 1800s offered a universe of discourse and strategy for black education, economic improvement, political empowerment, cultural enrichment, and mutual assistance (Du Bois 1911:213–14; Wilmore 1983:78–98).

The Expansion of Black Storefront Churches in Chicago

Before and after the Civil War, black dreams, visions, hopes, and strategies for social justice and equality were kept alive in black churches in the South and in the urban North. Between 1850 and 1930 Chicago's black population increased from 323 to 233,903 (Spear 1967:12). Black migrants moved North to escape rural economic destitution, Jim Crow laws, and white brutality. They hoped for steady work, an improved standard of living, and social mobility. In Chicago, black aspirations for equality were cut short by white racism and economic and political power (Spear 1967:29–49). Blacks encountered economic subordination, job discrimination, and de facto segregation in the city. Hostile and powerful whites forced blacks to settle in enclaves apart from white residential areas. White racists demanded segregated schools, neighborhoods, recreational facilities, and public accommodations (Spear 1967; Anderson and Pickering 1986).

In the urban North, the black church no longer served as the preeminent agency for organizing black protest. Alongside black churches there were black political leaders, entrepreneurs, educators, lawyers, doctors, and journalists who defined and represented black issues and interests. In the early 1900s, black response to white discrimination and demands for segregation was divided. One group of black leaders in Chicago believed it was in their interest to accommodate white demands for separate institutions. They were aligned with a movement led by Booker T. Washington, who articulated an ideology of racial solidarity and black self-help. They were opposed by another group of black civic leaders who believed in black equality and integration. This group was aligned with the Niagara Movement, a national organization led by W. E. B. Du Bois to oppose Booker T. Washington and segregation. The followers of Du Bois also supported the National Association for the Advancement of Color People (NAACP), an organization founded to struggle for equal rights for blacks. While the NAACP succeeded in breaking down legal barriers that were restricting black civil rights, Morris (1984:12–16) argued, the organization did not represent the black masses or directly address the economic exploitation of blue-collar black workers.

Although whites failed to pass segregation laws, a de facto color line was established in the early 1900s in Chicago that was not challenged until the modern Civil Rights movement in the 1950s. Black institutions in Chicago developed in a social context defined by racism and the black struggle for economic opportunities and equal rights. Until the 1950s, low- and middle-income blacks were concentrated in segregated and overcrowded neighborhoods, had restricted job opportunities, and attended inferior public schools (Spear 1967; Anderson and Pickering 1986). In the racist social climate of the early 1900s in Chicago, blacks were not allowed to attend white churches; several white churches posted signs notifying them to stay away (Drake 1940).

Class consciousness and aspirations for social mobility in the early 1900s divided black Christians. Established black middle-class churches with the capacity for more members did not attract poor black migrants who flooded into Chicago between 1910 and 1930. In churches dominated by black middle-class interests, poor blacks felt uncomfortable and unwelcome. The reserved manner of black middle-class congregants and the formal and staid conduct of worship services in these churches did not appeal to poor black settlers (Daniel 1940; Drake 1940). Poor Southern blacks wanted churches in which they could feel and express the presence and power of God with their voices and bodies during devotional services. For them, church was also a place to meet others as equals and to develop social ties based on common spiritual identity. For low-income blacks, church provided opportunities to gain social and spiritual status through church service and stewardship. Poor blacks avoided established middle-class churches, where they could not compete for prestigious positions (Daniel 1942; Drake and Cayton 1945; Mays and Nicholson 1969). According to Drake (1940:203–7) the majority of black settlers did not have sufficient resources for clothing and church dues to participate in middle-class churches and were driven into storefront congregations, where extreme poverty did not prevent them from assuming prestigious church vocations.

As blacks settled in Chicago, independent churches flowered. By 1930 blacks had established five hundred churches; approximately three hundred of them were located in converted storefronts (Sutherland 1928; Drake 1940; Drake and Cayton 1945). Storefront churches were established by small groups of people united by shared spiritual beliefs and practices and by common social and class origins. Many of Chicago's large present-day black congregations started in modest storefronts in the early 1900s. As these congregations grew and their members moved into the middle class, they secured funds and moved into conventional church buildings. Since the late 1800s, the storefront church has been independently owned and managed by working-class blacks. In the early 1900s the storefront church addressed an institutional hiatus in the "black belt" by providing a forum in which oppressed blacks could voice social problems apart from white control. They owned the church and determined the rules that governed them there. In the storefronts they developed leaders who could speak about their issues in a way that made sense to them.

The first black churches founded in Chicago in the mid-1800s, Quinn Chapel A.M.E. and Olivet Baptist Church, organized black protest and black social welfare movements. Quinn Chapel and Olivet B.C. were founded by small prayer bands that originally met in private homes and then moved to abandoned storefronts. Both churches moved into traditional church buildings as the middle-class base in each church expanded (Drake 1940). The black issues addressed in these churches before the Civil War included the problem of fugitive slaves—members of these churches worked the underground railroad—abolition; black adult literacy; and the education of black ministers and construction of churches, for which they held fund-raising drives (Drake 1940). By the early 1900s Olivet B.C. and Quinn Chapel sponsored boys' and girls' clubs, athletic activities, literary societies, relief programs, a reading room and library, a savings bank, and an employment bureau (Spear 1967:92). A wider range of social outreach programs was offered at Chicago's Institutional Church and Settlement House, founded in 1900 by Rev. Reverdy Ransom. Institutional Church provided a day nursery; a kindergarten; an employment bureau; a print shop; a gymnasium; and sewing, cooking, and music classes (Spear 1967:95). For twenty years Institutional Church attracted poor blacks who benefited from its social programs. Middle-class blacks were drawn by Rev. Ransom's reform ideology and his leadership and activism for black equality and integration.

Thus black churches in Chicago have provided a forum for defining black moral and social purpose, as the independent black churches in the South began to do earlier, and their members have sought through these bodies to improve their daily lives while addressing the larger social issues of black liberation and equal rights.

CHAPTER TWO

The Setting

While the Civil Rights movement ended legal segregation in the South and secured political rights for blacks, it did not end de facto segregation, racism, and uneven economic development for working-class blacks in American cities (Marable 1983:23–67), of which Chicago is a good example. The founders of First Corinthians M.B.C. and individuals who joined the church in the 1950s and early 1960s were southern immigrants who moved to Chicago in pursuit of jobs and social mobility. They were without property, unskilled, poorly educated, and strictly dependent on the city's blue-collar labor market. As some of their life histories show, their hopes for steady work and economic and social betterment were shattered by the devastating decline in Chicago's blue-collar industry and by the concomitant fragmentation of black institutions in the inner city over the past twenty years. In the biblical narratives articulated in worship services, prayer and healing meetings, and Bible study at First Corinthians, members find some redress for the harshness and inequities of ghetto life.

First Corinthians is located in Garfield Park, on Chicago's West Side, and serves both that community and the contiguous one of Austin. Most of its members live in these communities. The disfiguring signs of economic underdevelopment abound on the streets of Austin and Garfield Park, two among the seventeen community areas in Chicago that have been impoverished and predominantly black since the late 1960s (Wilson 1987:20–62). The West Side of Chicago was first settled in the mid-1850s by Scandinavian, Polish, German, and Irish immigrants. They lived in frame houses near railroad lines and worked in railroads yards and factories along the railroad. In the mid-1890s, improvements in local transportation, cheap land values, and new waves of European migration led to rapid commercial and residential growth (Chicago Fact Book

Consortium 1984:66–75). The West Side remained multiethnic and middle-class through the 1950s, when it changed rapidly with an influx of black migrants from the South. Racially segregated residential areas in Chicago had been created in the early 1900s and maintained by powerful whites who discriminated against blacks and controlled the city's government and distribution of public resources (Spear 1967; Katznelson 1973; Anderson and Pickering 1986). Many whites, driven by fear that the value of their property would decline when blacks moved in, left their neighborhoods as this began to happen; within ten years forty thousand whites moved out of Austin and Garfield Park, and sixty thousand blacks moved in (Chicago Fact Book Consortium 1984:69–72).

The black masses settling on the West Side were seeking jobs in the city's blue-collar labor market and a better standard of living than they could have achieved in the South. Throughout the 1970s, however, Chicago's manufacturing industry sharply declined and left a massive number of blue-collar workers jobless and welfare-dependent (Wilson 1987:100–106). This economic decline was the consequence of several factors: the relocation of manufacturing industries away from central cities to suburbs and to other nations, technological innovation, and the shift from a goods-producing to a service-producing economy (Wilson 1987:39–46). The steady loss of blue-collar jobs has resulted in an overall rise in unemployment in Chicago, and blacks and other minorities who depend on such jobs have been the hardest hit.

These structural changes in the urban economy have expanded joblessness, poverty, and welfare dependency among urban minorities since the 1960s. According to census data, in fifty cities in the United States the population living in poverty increased 12 percent between 1970 and 1980 (Wilson 1987:46). In this period, over 50 percent of the nation's poor live in five cities—Los Angeles, Detroit, Philadelphia, Chicago, and New York—in neighborhoods that are apart from the middle class (Wilson 1987:46). While the population has decreased by 9 percent in these cities, the population living in poverty in them has increased 22 percent. The poor black population in these cities has increased 164 percent (Wilson 1987:46–47).

In Chicago, poverty—especially among blacks—spread between 1970 and 1980. By 1980, 25 percent of Chicago's population was living in poverty; 62 percent of the city's poor are black (City of Chicago, Department of Planning 1982). In 1970 sixteen of Chicago's seventy-seven community areas were in poverty; by 1980 ten more community areas were in poverty (Wilson 1987:50). By 1980 Austin was 73 percent black, with 28 percent of the black population in poverty (Public Service Report Series Number Two, Selected 1980 Census 1983). Most of Austin's poor blacks are concentrated in the southwest part, which shares a boundary with Garfield Park. In the same period, Garfield Park was 98 percent black, with 71 percent in poverty (Public Service Report Series Number Two, Selected 1980 Census 1983).

In Austin and Garfield Park the unemployment rate in the 1980s reached 18 percent—50 percent greater than the national rate for that period (Mayor's Office of Employment and Training, 1979–1982). In these communities approximately 50 percent of the black population over sixteen years old is not in the labor force, and over 50 percent relies on public assistance (City of Chicago, Department of Planning 1983). Employment prospects for black teenagers in Chicago's inner city are diminished by inadequate public schools, described as the "worst in the Nation" by Secretary of Education William Bennett in the mid-1980s. Over half of the black students enrolled in Chicago's public schools drop out; a significant proportion of the ones who do graduate cannot read above the eighth-grade level. These students are not prepared to continue their education or to compete for jobs in the city's service economy (Wilson 1987:57–58). A significant number of inner-city blacks—especially young black males—are involved in crime and are in prison (Wilson 1987:22–26; Marable 1983:105–30). Death from violent crime and random shootings is a continual threat in these neighborhoods (Wilson 1987:22–26).

As poverty, joblessness, and occupational despair spread in schools and workplaces, life chances for individuals and families in black inner-city neighborhoods eroded. A study carried out by the mayor's office in 1984 indicated that Austin and Garfield Park are among seventeen community areas that are medically underserved because of manpower shortages (City of Chicago, Health Systems Agency 1984). In 1984 a report on hunger issued by the mayor's office indicated that over 50 percent of the people in Austin and Garfield Park were in serious risk from food shortages (City of Chicago, Report of the Mayor's Task Force on Hunger 1984). The same report stated that the seventy soup kitchens and pantries distributing food in Austin and Garfield Park were insufficient to serve the vast number of people there who lacked adequate food supplies. A nutrition survey carried out at Cook County Hospital, which provides care to the city's poor, showed that 90 percent of the infants examined in the hospital's clinics had nutritional deficiencies.[1] The total infant mortality rate in Chicago between 1979 and 1982 was 39 percent: 13 percent among whites and 26 percent among blacks. In the same period, infant mortality in Austin and Garfield Park was 26 percent (City of Chicago, *Report on the Mayor's Task Force on Hunger* 1984).

Economic dislocations and hardship are evident throughout the six-mile stretch that Austin and Garfield Park cover, as they are in other locations in the city with large impoverished populations. There are many boarded-up factories, condemned apartment buildings, and vacant commercial premises. Public buildings, streets, and residential quarters are in need of extensive repairs. Broken windows covered with plastic, gang graffiti, wrecked pavements, and litter are pervasive on all but a few streets. There was substantial damage to commercial properties during race riots that spread through the area in the 1960s. Many buildings that were burned and looted in the riots have not been restored. While several businesses closed in the aftermath of the rioting, others stayed in business, installing gates on their fronts and hiring private-duty guards. Crime against businesses is high on the West Side, however, and people in the neighborhood pay higher costs for everyday goods and services.

Main thoroughfares in Austin and Garfield Park abound in carryout restaurants, laundromats, game rooms, bars, liquor stores, corner grocery stores, variety shops, barber shops, beauty salons, record stores, and used auto part and tire-repair shops; these are also important locations for sociability (Hannerz 1969; Anderson 1978; Liebow 1967). In warm weather there is much commercial and social activity on the streets. Vendors sell their wares from blankets or tables set on pavements, in front yards, and in abandoned lots; some carry their goods to crowded intersections on pushcarts, pickup trucks, and station wagons. Typical items for sale on these streets include refreshments, jewelry, household goods, clothing, accessories, and fortune-enhancing charms. The market for inexpensive fast foods here is good, and there is a large supply of vendors catering to it. In abandoned lots barbecue stands are set up. Large metal barrels are used for grilling pork ribs, hot dogs, Polish sau-

---

1. I received this information in April 1986 from Cook County Hospital physicians when I lectured there on the decline of breast- feeding among low-income black women.

sage, pork skins, and corn. There are plenty of pushcart stands selling snow cones—crushed ice with fruit flavoring syrup—an inexpensive treat popular among children.

There is considerable crime on these streets, and people who live in the neighborhood are afraid of strangers. Outdoor refreshment stands are among the few locales where they let their guard down and engage in small talk with other people they know. For small children, teens, and women, visits to refreshment stands and the corner grocer are ongoing through the day. For women with children, these outings are a break from the daily routines of cleaning, child care, and cooking, a chance to visit with neighbors and hear the news going around the neighborhood. The streets, bars, game rooms, and carryout shops are locations of sociability for unemployed men and teenage boys who have dropped out of school and are without jobs.[2] While the streets are a gathering and visiting place for some in the neighborhood, however, others—especially church affiliated individuals—loathe the street scene. Many believe that by participating in street life, a person loses respectability and risks becoming a victim of crime.

The declining socioeconomic conditions in Austin and Garfield Park represent the state of affairs in other black urban neighborhoods. Decades of de facto segregation, joblessness, poverty, and public indifference have disfigured and ruined these areas. Throughout the 1980s public hostility toward the inner city heightened. In this decade, the gap between the rich and the poor increased. From the perspective of political and economic elites who controlled public policy in that period, poverty resulted from individual moral collapse; the poor in the inner city had only themselves to blame for their lot. As President Ronald Reagan's administration led the charge to drastically cut the budget for social programs in the early 1980s, his administration put the onus on the poor to reverse their destiny by sharing in the principles of self-help and self-reliance. The official ideology of blaming victims for their life chances overlooked the practical limitations of subsisting on low wages and inadequate welfare payments, which have left individuals and families destitute in the inner city. Political and economic elites denied that the industrial economy on which the working class depended failed before

---

2. Hannerz (1969), Liebow (1967), and Rose (1987) have discussed the world of black male street life. See Anderson (1978) for a discussion of a neighborhood bar and social relationships among low-income black men.

they had a chance to accumulate capital to join the ranks of the middle class. Under Reagan and his successor, George Bush, social conditions in inner-city neighborhoods worsened. These administrations failed to deliver public resources for badly needed basic human services and for economic revitalization in black ghettoes.[3]

---

3. See Marable (1983), Wilson (1987), and Lemann (1991) for analyses of public policy and the urban poor in the United States.

CHAPTER THREE

The Founding of First Corinthians Missionary Baptist Church

First Corinthians Missionary Baptist Church was founded by Rev. James Thomas and the group he mobilized around him in his early years in Chicago in the late 1940s. Rev. Thomas is six feet two inches tall and husky. He comports himself with an air of dignity and seriousness. He is gregarious and takes a personal interest in every member of the congregation. The growth of First Corinthians M.B.C.'s congregation from twenty-six people to over three hundred is largely the result of his business acumen, energy, tenacity, persuasive ability, and vocal talent. Rev. Thomas says God blessed him to lead First Corinthians M.B.C. His blessings include a group of people who he believes were destined by God to help him build a successful church.

Rev. Thomas and most evangelical ministers who established store-front churches in his generation are poorly educated. They are rural southern immigrants who lack formal theological training, and they rely on what they believe are God's gifts (charisma) to guide their ministry (Sutherland 1928; Drake 1940; Drake and Cayton 1945; Williams 1974; Frazier 1974; Paris 1984). Weber provided a model for interpreting the religious vocations of these ministers in his discussion of the prophet, salvation, and charisma (Weber 1978: 439–40). According to his view, prophets are legitimized by their personal calling and charismatic endowment—unlike priests, who hold office by virtue of their training in a sacred tradition. In Weber's schema, prophets are instructed by God. They have the ability to directly receive God's word, which reveals his plan for humanity's salvation. For Weber, the prophet's divine revelations embody a system of moral and ethical knowledge. Weber also suggests that the prophet's words and deeds articulate a view of the cosmos that meaningfully orders natural and social calamities and encourages human beings in times of crisis and affliction. James Thomas's calling and the founding of First Corinthians M.B.C. follow the logic of Weber's conception of charismatic religious authority.

God Calls James Thomas to the Ministry

James Thomas was born in rural Mississippi in 1918.[1] His parents were not married. His father died before James Thomas was born, and his mother died when he was eight. He was reared by his mother's parents on the family farm in Mississippi. He left school in the third grade, unable to read and write. He says that the teacher of the one-room country school, four miles from his home, promoted him because of his size. He worked on his grandparents' farm until he was nine, when he got a job working on the railroad carrying water, spikes, and planks for $2.48 a day. In 1929 Thomas's family was unable to keep the bank from taking the farm. That year he was hired to plough fields in Alabama for $10 a month, including board and transportation. His earnings from these jobs were paid to his grandparents to help support the family; James Thomas's grandmother gave him a small allowance from his salary. After two seasons, he left Alabama for Baton Rouge, Louisiana. There he worked on the railroad for 18 cents an hour until he met a man named Slim, who hired him to drive a truck for 50 cents an hour. James Thomas and Slim became friends and spent time together after work. In Baton Rouge, Thomas became a successful professional gambler. From his earnings he bought a saloon and cafeteria. His girlfriend operated the business while he drove trucks for Slim and gambled.

After he had been in Baton Rouge for twelve years, Thomas said, his luck ran out. He was in serious trouble with other gamblers and with the women he was courting. He sold the business in a rush and headed for St. Louis to stay with kin and begin a new life, but he failed to find work there, and within a month he had lost most of his money gambling. He got on a Greyhound bus headed for Chicago, with, as he said, "$1.65 in my pocket and the address of some kins who lived in the city."

---

1. This account of Rev. James Thomas's life and calling is based on three tape-recorded interviews I conducted during my field work and on biographical anecdotes I recorded from his sermons.

He sees the series of misfortunes that start in Baton Rouge and trail him on his way north as the beginning of his calling to the ministry. As he put it, "When God wants a feller to do his work, he has a way of tightening down on him and bringing him to his knees."

For James Thomas, this moment came in the early morning of June 9, 1947, on the Greyhound bus from St. Louis. As the bus coasted into Chicago, he watched the sun rise over Lake Michigan. Thomas said that the image of "the great big red sun coming out of the lake was the most beautiful thing I'd ever seen." As he watched the sunrise on the lake, he suddenly felt a change come over him. He could feel that there was something very important for him to do in the city. On the bus, for the first time in his adult life, he prayed, asking God to save him from gambling, drinking, and womanizing. He asked God to help him find a way to settle in Chicago.

James Thomas was reared in a Christian family. His grandmother was deeply religious and concerned with her family's salvation. In their rural community in Mississippi, church services were conducted by itinerant ministers one Sunday a month, which was known as pastoral day. Thomas's grandparents had made him attend Sunday School and Sunday worship services, but he was not interested in what the visiting preachers had to say or in the church. Nevertheless, at the age of twelve, he confessed his faith in Christ and was baptized in a river near his church. Although he had been baptized, he said, he was considered a mean and stupid child and a bad Christian in his rural community, and adults feared and despised him. They did not expect him to amount to much, and they did not allow him to court girls. The religious principles he had learned from his community church and his family had no place in his life until the morning he came to Chicago and felt God's presence.

In Chicago, Thomas took streetcars to the home of his relatives, getting directions from strangers along the way. In nine days he got a job loading trucks in a foundry. He earned $85 a week, which was more than the other males in the family earned. To help himself avoid gambling shops and taverns, he organized a gospel quartet among the men in the household. That year he met Leon Simms, who took him to his first church service in Chicago. They went to the Rock of Ages Baptist Church, located in a storefront on the West Side. Thomas joined the church and was soon elected a deacon. He arranged for his gospel quartet to sing at the church. He asked the men in the quartet to join Rock of Ages and become active in its affairs in order to strengthen their posi-

tion there against competing gospel groups. But his request led everyone except his cousin T. C. Robertson to leave the group. It took Thomas
two years to organize a new, larger group, which contained, in addition
to Thomas and Robertson, three pairs of brothers he had met in other
storefront churches in the city. He named the group the Heavenly Knights
and became their manager. This group and members of their families
joined Rock of Ages Baptist Church.

James Thomas married in 1949. He met his wife, Sarah Hanks, on a
singing tour with the Heavenly Knights in Jackson, Mississippi. Sammie
Willis, one of the Heavenly Knights, arranged to visit Sarah Hanks's
home; Sarah is the sister of his best friend, Lester Hanks, with whom he
had sung in a quartet—the Melodious Kings—in the 1940s before Sammie
Willis and his brother joined the Heavenly Knights. During the visit,
Thomas decided that Sarah was the woman he would marry. He returned to Jackson a few weeks later to propose to her. He explained that
he did not want another girlfriend and that he did not want to court. He
wanted a wife who would not mind his work in the church. Sarah had
grown up in a religious family and had always been affiliated with a
church, so she had no objections to his religious interests. They married
in Jackson, and Sarah moved to Chicago and joined Rock of Ages Baptist Church. Now at First Corinthians Missionary Baptist Church, she is
called mother and first lady of the church. Some congregants say that
while Rev. Thomas does all the "hooting and hollering, mother is
pastoring the church." The Thomases have two daughters; both are single
parents. The older daughter is the church organist, and the younger is
in the Gospel Choir. Lester Hanks and his wife Doris joined First
Corinthians M.B.C. when they moved to Chicago in the 1950s. They are
deacon and deaconess in the church. Hanks continues to sing with the
Melodious Kings, and the group often performs at First Corinthians
M.B.C.

The Heavenly Knights Establish a Church

For a year James Thomas managed to book performances for the Heavenly Knights in Rock of Ages Baptist Church, but after several disputes
with the church pastor over the use of the church for rehearsals and
performances by competing gospel groups, he, the Heavenly Knights,
and eighteen other congregants left Rock of Ages to start another church.
Under Thomas's direction, the group rented a second-floor loft that was

parallel to the elevated train tracks on Lake Street on Chicago's West Side. They held their first meeting in this loft on May 15, 1950, to elect church officers. Fifteen people were present. The meeting started with Sister Nancy Willis singing "Jesus Keep Me Near the Cross." Rev. Ben Jacobs offered a prayer after her song. He was followed by Thomas, who read the Twenty-third Psalm and then sang his song "I Wonder If the Light from the Lighthouse Will Shine on Me?" Ever since then, at First Corinthians M.B.C. the congregation begins worship every Sunday morning by reciting the Twenty-third Psalm, and Rev. James Thomas sings this song as he opens the doors of the church for individuals to come forward to confess a hope in Christ and become members of First Corinthians.

On the agenda at the first church meeting was naming the church, electing church officers, and setting the date for the first church service. James Thomas proposed a name for the church in the form of a motion that was seconded by Nancy Willis and J. C. Tylor. Rev. Ben Jacobs was elected pastor. Thomas was elected deacon and superintendent of the Sunday School. Nancy Willis was elected president of the Pastor's Aid Committee. T. C. Tylor was elected trustee. Anthony Carter was elected deacon, church clerk, and Sunday School teacher. Angie Darling was elected president of the Baptist Training Union. The group decided to hold the first church service on July 23, 1950.

First Corinthians M.B.C. grew rapidly in the 1950s and 1960s; new members were drawn largely from the southern relatives of the church's founding members. For the first fifteen years at First Corinthians, James Thomas was an influential deacon and church leader. His main concern during those years, however, was to manage the Heavenly Knights. With a home church, the group had a place to rehearse and perform regularly. In 1952 Thomas met the owner of a recording studio in which the Heavenly Knights cut a record. With a church and a record, they became better known on the West Side. They received frequent bookings to perform in other storefront churches in Chicago and were regularly invited to sing in Detroit and in Jackson, Mississippi.

The Heavenly Knights were in their late twenties and thirties when they met. They had come from the South and worked in blue-collar jobs in the city. All of these men describe themselves as having been corrupted by excessive drinking, gambling, and womanizing by the time they met each other in the storefront churches. Since 1949 the Heavenly Knights have been inseparable (though two of the singers died in the

1970s). Lasting friendships have also been made among the men's spouses, children, and grandchildren, who have shared experiences in the church. Among the Heavenly Knights singers and their families there have been considerable affliction, domestic problems, joblessness, and serious financial difficulties. They have relied on each other in times of hardship, shared amusements and hospitality, helped each other find spouses, and established a church in which members of the second and third generations of their families participate.

In 1962 the Heavenly Knights Juniors Gospel Quartet was formed. Except for Don Williams, the men in this group are related by blood to members of the original Heavenly Knights. Williams is a boyhood friend of Jesse Larson, who is the only son of Rev. Charles Larson, a member of the Heavenly Knights and an assistant minister at First Corinthians M.B.C. In 1981 a second Heavenly Knights Junior group was organized among the males in the third generation: Don Williams's son Darrel Williams is in this group. A female gospel group, the Larson Singers, was organized in 1972 among women related to the Heavenly Knights. Rev. Charles Larson is their manager. The Larson Singers and the Heavenly Knights Juniors sing often at First Corinthians M.B.C.; they also sing at other storefront churches around Chicago and take annual trips to sing in Mississippi, Alabama, and Missouri.

During its first fifteen years, First Corinthians M.B.C. relocated five times and had two pastors. It remained in the Lake Street loft for five years. In 1955 the church moved to a second-floor apartment on Racine Street. Three years later it moved to a storefront on Madison Street. In 1963 the congregation was evicted from Madison Street because Rev. Ben Jacobs did not pay the rent. The majority of the congregation believed that Jacobs appropriated church funds, and he was forced to resign. Jacobs and his supporters left First Corinthians M.B.C. and founded another church in a one-room storefront on the West Side.

In the midst of the disorganization brought on by the congregation's eviction and the resignation of the church pastor, James Thomas moved the church into another storefront on Washington Street and persuaded the group to elect Paul Samuels church pastor. Rev. Samuels led the church for two years before he became seriously ill. On his sickbed, he told Thomas that he would have to take the church over. Since the beginning of his career as a gospel singer in Chicago's storefront churches, Thomas had inspired audiences. People told him that he was a born preacher and that they came to hear him preach as much as they came to hear him sing. At first, Thomas was not interested in the ministry. He says that he was not ready to "turn away from the world to turn toward God." For years he had held a low opinion of preachers; he said that he viewed them as "men who took old folks' money, courted lots of women, and went around buying Cadillacs." Thomas wanted to be a gospel singer and to do evangelical work. For eighteen years before his calling, he managed the Heavenly Knights, sang gospel, worked in the church as deacon, and loaded trucks in the foundry to support his family.

James Thomas's calling to the ministry was hastened in 1965, when, he said, "God once again cut off my blessings and brought me to my knees." Through the 1950s, the Heavenly Knights were a success. They had a record; they sang weekly at First Corinthians M.B.C.; and they enjoyed regular bookings around Chicago, Detroit, and the South. In the 1960s, however, bookings became rare, and on several occasions the group did not get the money it had been promised for a performance. That was also the time when church funds were stolen, the congregation was evicted, and there was a lack of leadership. With these troubles in the church, Thomas said, he knew that God was again "tightening down" on him. Things got worse before he yielded, however. In February 1965, his home caught on fire while he was at work. Sarah and the children escaped uninjured, but the house was destroyed, and the family moved in with Thomas's relatives. He prayed to God to provide a new home. He also told God that he was ready to answer his call.

For a few months, Thomas continued to sing and manage the group until one night in the church at the Washington Street location, the Heavenly Knights were to sing in an evening church program. For several months before this evening, the congregation had been praying for a leader and for church stability. After reciting Scripture and "talking up" his song, Thomas "missed it." As he explained it, he can sing gospel only when the Holy Spirit inspires him. That night he could not "connect with the Spirit" and had to sit down. That was the first time in seventeen years that he had not "hit a song." At that moment, another member of the group, Jack Simms, was told by the Holy Spirit that God was calling James Thomas to the ministry. The Holy Spirit swept through the congregation; there was considerable shouting as the congregation felt that God was calling Thomas to lead First Corinthians M.B.C. By the end of the night, Thomas testified and was ordained.

After his ordination, Rev. Thomas stopped singing with the Heavenly Knights and managing the group; Nel Gibson became its booking manager. Thomas joined the Assistant Ministers Board until September of that year, when he was elected pastor. At that time, he did not believe he had the ability to lead the church. He saw himself as a man who had had a checkered career, lacked patience, had a mean disposition, and was poorly educated—he had taught himself to read and write in his late thirties with the help of a woman friend in Chicago. On the way home from one of the first meetings he led as church pastor, he took his doubts to God in his parked car. God told Rev. Thomas he had been training him since 1947 for this job and that he had taught him how to treat people right—which, God said, was the most important thing he needed to know. That night God also told Rev. Thomas that he would send people to help him pastor the church.

The People God Sent to
First Corinthians M. B. C.

The men and women who founded First Corinthians M.B.C. in 1950 in the loft on Lake Street and others who joined the church in the early years are staunch supporters of Rev. James Thomas and the church.[2] Church members believe that First Corinthians is sustained through their God-given abilities to work for the church, and some of them have played a significant role in shaping the beliefs and routines of First Corinthians M.B.C.

Rev. Charles Larson and Linda Larson have been members of First Corinthians since the church was founded. They were among the small group of people who cleaned and furnished the storefronts, gave money to the church, and recruited new members in its early years. Rev. Larson met Rev. Thomas at a storefront church in Chicago in 1949 one evening after a gospel music program in which he sang with his brother Leon Larson. Rev. Thomas liked their singing and asked both men to join the Heavenly Knights. They accepted his offer. Charles Larson and James Thomas have been inseparable companions since their first meeting. Leon Larson stayed with the Heavenly Knights until the early 1970s, when he left the group and dropped his church affiliation. He spent his last days in the Veterans Administration Hospital and was given a funeral at First Corinthians M.B.C. in 1982.

---

2. The life histories discussed in this section are based on tape-recorded interviews I conducted with these individuals during my field work.

Rev. Charles Larson is the eldest of eleven children born to a Mississippi farm family, and he was the first in his family to leave Mississippi. He and his wife, who was also born in rural Mississippi, settled in Chicago with their three children in 1946. Larson found a job in a factory on the West Side operating a punch press machine. Linda Larson found domestic work in a suburb near Chicago. Through the 1950s the Larsons had steady work and saved enough money to buy a car and a two-story building in a West Side neighborhood they considered a decent place to live and raise their children. Since 1952 they have given money and hard work to support the church. Both of the Larsons had lived in poverty in rural Mississippi, where they had no opportunities to earn a decent living and support a family. They had also grown up in families in which "God and the Bible ruled." In the early years of their marriage, when they were still in Mississippi and struggling just to put food on the table, they never stopped believing in and worshiping God. In their view, the work they found in the North, their property, and their car were all God-given blessings. Though their fortunes have since fallen, they still believe that God expects them to give back to him through their support for the church.

Charles Larson was ordained in 1967 and is an assistant minister. Linda Larson sits on the influential and prestigious Pastors Aid Committee and on the Senior Mothers Board. The Larsons' chief contribution to First Corinthians M.B.C. has been the people they attracted to the church. Their two daughters, Annie Larson and Jackie Evans, and their spouses and children are active members of the congregation. The Larsons' only son, Jesse Larson, is also a member of the church. Jesse Larson's wife, Elsa, is a member of another church. She comes to First Corinthians M.B.C. for special church events; their five children attend services and programs in both churches. In addition to these relatives, there are fifty-seven other people in the church who are related to Linda and Charles Larson. Their relatives migrated from Mississippi in the 1950s and 1960s and stayed with them until they could settle in their own places. As their relatives arrived from the South, Linda and Charles Larson introduced them to First Corinthians M.B.C.

The Larsons' relatives are among Rev. James Thomas's strongest supporters in the church; they serve on several committees and boards and collectively make a substantial financial contribution to the church. Rev. Larson's nephew, Deacon B. J. Clark, is the chairman of the Deacon Board. He has a good income from a construction job. For twenty-seven years he has made significant financial contributions to the church. He is also unwavering in his support of Rev. Thomas. Deacon Clark, his wife, Ann Clark, and their five children are active church members. Ann Clark is a registered nurse and a member of the Deaconess Board. She and her husband are a couple whom others turn to for advice and seek to emulate. Deacon Clark also manages the Heavenly Knights Juniors and is highly respected by the group. They see him as a role model for the younger men in the group and the church.

Linda and Charles Larson have made a way of life for themselves that is centered on First Corinthians M.B.C. They, like other senior church members, are proud of the accomplishments of Rev. Thomas and their church. At First Corinthians the Larsons have established lasting friendships with people on whom they can rely. While the Larsons prospered in Chicago in the 1950s and the early 1960s, they presently live in poverty and hardship; their church and family are sources of comfort, assistance, and respectability. In the late 1960s race riots spread throughout their neighborhood. Businesses near their home were burned and looted. Throughout the 1970s businesses and factories in their neighborhood shut down, and unemployment grew among their family members and members of the church.

In 1974 Rev. Larson injured his back on his job. He has been unable to work since then. For two years after the accident Linda Larson supported him while he struggled to get a settlement from the company and Social Security benefits. After what the Larsons considered much humiliation and harassment from government and company officials, he got a five-thousand-dollar settlement from his job and a monthly disability check from the government. He described the government and company representatives who handled his claim this way: "They treated me like I was trying to get out of a job. Didn't matter to them that I had been on that job and worked hard for twenty-two years. All of a sudden they start looking at me like I was trying to get something for nothing. That hurts me more than the pain in this here back of mine."

To add to their hardship, Linda Larson became critically ill in 1981. She collapsed at work and was taken to Cook County Hospital, where she was diagnosed with heart disease and told that she would be unable to work for the rest of her life. Linda was in the hospital for two weeks and convalesced at home for three months. She then returned to her job. Although she was fatigued and in pain, she managed to go to her job for a few months until she became ill again and went back to the hospital. She was seriously underweight, anemic, and disoriented. When she was discharged from the hospital this time, she attempted to return to her job but was too weak to continue. She has no employee benefits and has been unable to get Social Security payments.

When I met Linda and Charles Larson in 1981, their building was run-down; they did not have money to maintain the property and were just managing to pay the monthly utility bills. There are several abandoned buildings on their street that are hangouts for local gangs. They are afraid in the neighborhood and are careful when going to and from their building. To help pay the bills and put some food on the table, they have taken in two boarders—Linda's nephew Bob and Charles's aunt Priscilla. Bob works in a factory; Priscilla is seventy-three and gets Social Security benefits. Linda shops, cooks, and cleans for the household. Priscilla is diabetic and thus requires additional care. Since Linda Larson's last hospitalization, caring for the boarders is a burden she would rather not have, but she and her husband could not manage financially without them.

By going to First Corinthians M.B.C. the Larsons get away from the isolation and drudgery of their home. Rev. Larson gets to church early on Sunday and stays there the entire day. He also goes to church two or three evenings a week for Bible study, prayer meetings, and group rehearsals. As an assistant minister, he leads the congregation in prayer every Sunday morning, preaches when Rev. Thomas is away from the church, and drums up support for church programs—especially the ones sponsored by Rev. Thomas. Rev. Larson sings with the Heavenly Knights and manages the Larson Singers; with the gospel groups he gets around the city to perform at other storefront congregations and travels out of Chicago several times a year. Linda also gets to First Corinthians M.B.C. as often as possible. Since she became ill and started taking in the boarders, she has had to cut back her participation at First Corinthians M.B.C. Priscilla cannot be left in the house alone for more than a few hours and refuses to go to church. Linda makes it to morning worship service every Sunday and cooks and serves the church meal with other members of the Senior Mothers Board one Sunday a month. Although she has cut back some of her work on the Mission Circle, she still makes it to midweek prayer meeting and Bible study.

At First Corinthians M.B.C. Rev. Frank Dixon is remembered as a man whom God blessed with money and the heart to serve the church and the poor and downtrodden. Rev. Dixon met Rev. James Thomas in 1949 at Rock of Ages Baptist Church. He left Rock of Ages and went with the group that followed Rev. Thomas to establish First Corinthians. Rev. Dixon was called to the ministry in 1962. He was ordained at First Corinthians M.B.C. under Rev. Ben Jacobs and served on the church's Assistant Ministers Board for the rest of his life. Rev. Dixon was born in Louisiana in 1907. He married his wife, Melinda, in 1935. He was baptized in Little Rock, Arkansas, in 1955. Before he accepted Christ as his savior, he gambled for a living and was, according to his own description, a liar and a thief. He said, "When I gambled I could take your money right our from under you and you would never know it." In the late 1950s Rev. Dixon bought a building on Madison Street and began operating a prosperous soul food diner in its storefront. He and his wife and children lived in a flat above the diner. Church members say that throughout the 1950s and 1960s, Rev. Dixon was considered the richest man in the church. According to Rev. Thomas, Dixon always bailed the church out of serious financial trouble and kept its doors open. In the eyes of the congregation, his rejection of gambling and stealing was an act of God. As they see it, not only did God bless him with the power to make money that he could give to the church; he also gave him a heart that had room for everyone.

Rev. Dixon was deeply disturbed by the deprivation and suffering among members of his church and in the neighborhood in which he operated his business. As one congregant put it, "If he knew you was in trouble, he would do something for you." He gave money generously to the church and to his friends. For several members of First Corinthians M.B.C., their first job in Chicago was at his diner; there they earned some money and learned about the world. His diner was also a place where members of his church went to get a free meal when they did not have food and money, and he gave free meals to the homeless who roamed Madison Street. Rev. Dixon kept a Bible under the counter in the diner. He read it daily to himself and to his customers; he was especially enthusiastic about ministering to the homeless and troubled people who came in off the streets. His dream was to pastor a church, but he had lost one lung in his thirties from a bout of pneumonia and was unable to deliver a sermon. When he led the congregation in prayer from the pulpit, he could barely be heard.

In the last decade of his life Rev. Dixon lived in abject poverty. In his late sixties he became ill and was unable to keep his business open. He and his wife had no retirement benefits except for Social Security payments. Before his death, his household included his wife, their unwed daughter, her five children, and seven grandchildren from their youngest son, who had been killed in a gang fight. Their eldest son joined the army and did not return home. Their Social Security payments and their daughter's welfare payments were the only sources of income for the Dixon household. The Dixon property and other businesses on the block were sacked during the race riots. A few blocks from the diner, commercial and residential property was burned to the ground following the news of Dr. Martin Luther King's assassination. The neighborhood has not recovered from the loss. The diner was closed and boarded up, and the Dixons' building was run-down and rat infested like other buildings on that block. Rev. Dixon died in 1985 from colon cancer. When his disease was discovered, his physicians gave him less than a year to live; he lived for three more years. During those last three years he had several operations; he was confined to the hospital and his home much of the time. His participation in the church was limited to Sunday morning worship and the community meal following morning service. There he took his seat on the stage behind the pulpit with the other ministers. He wore three-piece suits and carried himself with dignity. He was always friendly and witty. Every time he returned, the spiritual sentiments were strong at First Corinthians M.B.C. For the congregation, every operation he overcame and every step he took beyond the time his doctors estimated he would live was a sign of Christ's healing power. Rev. Dixon, who was among the known saved who would spend eternity with God, was once again an instrument of God. In his affliction, operations, and remarkable recovery the congregation was witnessing God's power and mercy. They believed that God was using Rev. Dixon's body to build faith and unity in the church.

For thirty years Rev. Dixon provided financial support and ideas for developing the church program. Throughout those years he and Rev. Thomas were close companions. Dixon taught Thomas church management and finance; he showed him how to handle the accounts and motivate people to give money. It was Rev. Dixon's idea to build a kitchen in the church where meals would be served every Sunday. He set up the kitchen and taught church members to manage it; it now serves over two hundred free meals every Sunday. At Dixon's wake, Rev. Ben Jacobs, who had presided over his colleague's ordination thirty years earlier, called him one of the Lord's saints; he reminded the congregation that Rev. Dixon had renounced wealth and used his talents to work for God by serving the poor and the suffering.

Rev. Allen Tyson was the principal spiritual leader at First Corinthians M.B.C. for thirty-seven years. Rev. Tyson and his wife, Josephine, were among the group that founded First Corinthians in 1950. Church members considered Rev. Tyson the spiritual head of First Corinthians and called him "the Father of our church." Church members claim that, with the exception of two years in the early 1960s when Rev. Tyson left First Corinthians M.B.C. to start a church in another West Side storefront, he never missed a Sunday, a prayer meeting, or Bible study at First Corinthians M.B.C. Tyson served on the Assistant Ministers Board. According to Rev. Thomas, Allen Tyson was his spiritual mentor. Rev. Thomas said that God sent Rev. Tyson "to help me act right, temper my anger, teach me patience, and show me how to treat people right."

Tyson was born in Missouri in 1897. He died in Chicago in 1986. When we met, in 1981, he was five feet tall and frail. He tired easily and could not stand on his feet very long. In church he was friendly; he greeted people with a firm handshake while welcoming them to the house of the Lord. In the eyes of church members, Rev. Tyson's manner and dealings with other people provided an example of Christ's teachings. Tyson spoke with a firm voice. He was patient, kind, humble, and modest. He did not get angry or mistreat others. Above all, he had faith in God and love for humanity. He commanded respect in the church because of his spiritual demeanor. Angela Williams said, "I never saw a short black man get as much respect as Father Tyson did. When he said something to you, you'd listen. My brother Bernie would come in the church off the streets drunk, looking mean and unkept, and the big men in the church were afraid of him and would walk away. Father Tyson would go right up to him and say, 'Son, sit down and act right.' And Bernie would straighten up fast." Unlike other ministers at First Corinthians M.B.C., whom God saved from drinking, gambling, and womanizing, Rev. Tyson was reported by church members to have always walked with the Lord. Every Sunday morning during the worship service he would stand behind the pulpit and lead the congregation in reciting the Twenty-third Psalm. Sometimes the Spirit moved him, and he would preach a brief sermon. Although his voice was weak and he was difficult to hear, his presence at the pulpit elicited silence and respect.

A year after I met Rev. Tyson, his wife died. They had been married and inseparable for forty-three years. The Tysons were deeply respected among members of First Corinthians M.B.C. for the devotion, love, and kindness they had given to the church family. They had no children and had no extended family in Chicago. After Josephine Tyson's death, Allen Tyson lived in their one-bedroom apartment in a West Side public housing development. He lived on a modest Social Security check. Rev. Tyson never discussed his personal finances or church finances. He never owned real estate or a car. When Josephine died, he became less gregarious and grew melancholic; but through the concern and help of church members, he was sheltered from loneliness and despair. In the last few years of his life I often heard him say, "These days it is the Lord and this old church that keep me going." Besides being in church from 9:00 A.M. to 8:00 P.M. every Sunday, he went four evenings a week for Bible study, prayer meetings, and worship services. Church members took turns giving him a ride to and from church. Sarah Thomas called him every day to make sure he had food and medication. Like Rev. Dixon, he came to church dressed in a three-piece suit, and he was always carrying his Bible. Up to his last days at First Corinthians M.B.C., he continued to teach and preach the word of God.

According to Rev. James Thomas and other senior church members, all of these individuals were blessed by God with spiritual gifts and talents to support the church. While their personal and collective economic circumstances worsened and other social institutions failed them, their church continued to give meaning and structure to their lives. For the people who founded First Corinthians M.B.C. and those who joined later, the church is a refuge from the hardships and disorganization that mark their lives in the inner city and a place to restore their spirits. It is a place of love and acceptance, unlike the social world outside the church, where poor blacks are treated with suspicion, disrespect, condescension, and hostility. Within the congregation, individuals are honored and respected for their spiritual achievements, which are manifested in moral character development and the work they do for the church.

In Rev. Thomas's case, with his turn away from barroom vices, the good-paying job he found shortly after he arrived in Chicago, and his vocal talent, the group discerned a divine calling. Like the authority of the prophet in Weber's conception of charismatic religious authority, Rev. Thomas's authority rests on his and the group's belief in his charismatic endowment. Weber argued that charismatic religious groups are established by people who believe that divine spiritual dispensations shape individual and collective life; such groups, he held, have the intellectual and emotional capacity to discern charismatic qualities in individuals. At First Corinthians, these qualities have shaped church vocations, the structure of the organization, and church worship services.

CHAPTER FOUR

Church Cosmology and Organization

For members of First Corinthians M.B.C., God is an all-powerful being, a personal friend, and a savior.[1] In their conception God conquers evil, uncertainty, and death. According to their understanding of the enactment of God's relationship to humanity, they seek to rectify the conflicts between anger and mercy, greed and generosity, love and hate, and selfishness and sacrifice that in their view define human relationships. Their reach for God and eternal life involves a personal and collective struggle to overcome anger, greed, hate, and frustration over setbacks and social injustice. In their spiritual quest they seek moral character development based on the principles of love, mercy, and faith represented in their rendering of Christ's teachings and passion. The principles and practices enacted in First Corinthians M.B.C. resist and redefine socioeconomic inequality and white supremacy.

In the eyes of the congregation, when an individual joins the church, it is a sign of God's grace in that person's life. Members of First Corinthians M.B.C. believe that everyone who joins the church is blessed to work in the mission. Church principles give meaning and value to the volunteer work members do in the church and to their labor in the blue-collar market where they earn their living. The material values privileged in the American mainstream are subverted by the spiritual claim on money defined in church cosmology. In this congregation, having the ca-

---

1. The interpretive information in this chapter is based on tape-recorded Bible study sessions, sermons, and worship services and on tape-recorded interviews with church members over a three-year period.

pacity to work and having a job are considered divine gifts that lose their value if they are not returned to God through church stewardship.

Spiritual principles and social objectives inform the organization of space in the church building. The congregation uses the church space to create meaningful and ordered community activities. In its collective thought, the church is the house of God on earth, and relationships in the church must conform to their understanding of God's precepts.

God, the Devil, and Human Beings in the Cosmos

Members of First Corinthians M.B.C. share the hope that they will escape perdition through God's gift of everlasting life in his Kingdom in heaven. They conceive of God as omnipresent, omniscient, and omnipotent. God created the world and all things in the world, including humanity. He is a supreme being who rules over the world and humanity. Members of First Corinthians M.B.C. conceive of God as a triune being; he is the Father, the son Jesus, and the Holy Ghost. God the Father is the creator of all things in heaven and earth; he is called the "Boss man of this great universe." God came to earth and lived and walked among humanity as Jesus Christ, the Son of God. Christ came to show humanity that he has power to conquer evil and death and to teach humanity the word of God, which embodies his plan for salvation.

When Jesus completed his work on earth, God brought him back to heaven and returned as the Holy Ghost, also called the Spirit at First Corinthians M.B.C. The Holy Ghost, according to church members, is an active agent in day-to-day human affairs. The Holy Ghost imbues God's chosen people with spiritual gifts to serve God and humanity for their salvation. During Bible class Angela Williams explained the purpose of the Holy Ghost in human life this way: "Jesus told John when he was baptizing him that one more mightier than I will baptize you with the Holy Ghost. This is the fire that comes. This is the mover, the motivation, the worker, the guide, the teacher, the stimulant. This is what keeps us going. This is what sustains us. It is the comforter. It is your life. This is what holds us here to serve and save. Without this Holy Ghost fire we couldn't serve." Church members invoke the Holy Ghost in daily prayer to give them strength to endure and make sense of everyday life. They petition God the Father through the Holy Ghost in their private prayers and church prayer meetings for protection against evil and suffering.

According to church members, God created every human being with the potential to do evil, and he put humankind on earth, where evil and temptation abound. God creates and dispenses adversity in human life for divine purpose. In the members' schema, the devil, also called Satan, is the agent of evil and death. In their cosmology, the devil is controlled and dispatched by God for divine purpose. Church members believe that evil exists because Adam and Eve, the first man and woman God created, failed to obey him. Although God gave Adam and Eve everything they needed for a good life in heaven, they listened to the devil and disobeyed God. As Rev. James Thomas puts it, "Adam and Eve had plenty of good food and a nice place to live. All Adam had to do was to sit around and look at how pretty Eve was. All God wanted back was obedience. However, Adam and Eve let the devil lead them to temptation. God got angry at Adam and Eve and cast them out of heaven and condemned them to hell." After God banished Adam and Eve from heaven, he remained angry and did not want anything to do with humanity again. But because God is loving and merciful, he decided to give humanity another chance to reenter heaven by sacrificing himself.

Members of First Corinthians M.B.C. are united by their belief in the saving power of God through their faith and hope in the life, teachings, death, and resurrection of Jesus. He came to teach humanity the word of God and to show humanity God's power over the devil. God allowed the devil to use men to kill Jesus in a sinful and brutal way on the cross. While Jesus was suffering and dying on the cross, he did not lose faith in God the Father. Church members say that God let Jesus die on the cross, brought him back to life, and lifted him to heaven. In the collective thought of the congregation, God sacrificed himself by allowing men to ruthlessly kill Jesus to show humanity that he has the power to conquer evil and death. Through Jesus' death and resurrection, God has given humanity the opportunity to repent and be saved.

When Jesus returned to heaven, God left the devil behind to continue tempting humanity. But God returned to earth as the Holy Ghost to comfort, guide, and help individuals who believe in Jesus and who seek their salvation through his passion on the cross. Human beings are born sinners, but they are created with the capacity to discern right from wrong. Every individual must choose between God and the devil. Human beings experience and know God on earth through the Holy Ghost. Rev. Thomas says, "No matter how good you are or how good you think you are or how good you think you want to be, some kinda way or another the devil is going to get hold to you." According to members of First Corinthians M.B.C., the only hope that humanity has of overcoming evil is to believe in Jesus and to hope that God will save them. God in his mercy and love for humanity let the devil kill Jesus. While Jesus was dying on the cross, though, he did not lose faith in his Father. After Jesus died, God brought him back to life, and there was nothing the devil could do about it.

Members of First Corinthians M.B.C. await the day of rapture when Jesus will return to separate the righteous from the wicked. On that day, they say, with the twinkle of an eye Jesus will sweep a mighty wind over the land and lift the righteous up into the Kingdom, while sinners will be sent to eternal damnation. According to church members, individuals who are saved and have died are sleeping in their graves waiting for Jesus to come back on the day of rapture to take them home. They believe that all men are repenting sinners who have a chance to be saved by God's grace, embodied in the redemptive suffering, death, and resurrection of Jesus. Individuals who want to join the church must come to see themselves as sinners; they must repent and accept the teachings of Jesus. Church members believe they must be sincere about their intention to repent and be saved because God is all-knowing and cannot be deceived. In this cosmology God discerns an individual's intentions by examining the heart. God, they say, "reads your heart and knows everything about you." They believe that human beings receive God's gifts of faith, love, charity, knowledge, and prophetic wisdom through the heart. According to them, the devil tempts human beings to do evil by controlling their hearts. They believe that God reaches sinners by transforming their hearts.

According to church members, God, who creates all things for a purpose, made the church to give human beings on earth a place to learn about Jesus and about the word of God. At church individuals unite with others who believe in the redemptive death and resurrection of Jesus. While they believe that God has the power to save the worst sinner, they also believe that church-affiliated people have a better chance of being saved. At church the Holy Spirit gives individuals blessings in the form of divine revelations that strengthen their faith. Rev. Thomas explained the purpose of attending church this way:

> I think all of us are standing in the need of a blessing today. In fact that's why we come. We would that God would bless us. And he said that he would.

It is a blessing to come to church. You don't leave here with more money, maybe. But the spirit in you, within yourself, just enables you to go along a little better. So it's important to go to church. Because you'd be surprised how burdened you can get. You'd be surprised how many things you can see and can't do. You just don't have the spirit in you. And the spirit in us comes from God. We have to go where God wants us to come to. You just don't get it everywhere. Good as my living room looks, he just don't come there to bless me with what I need. But every time I come to church, I leave here feeling better. In fact, if I'm sick I'd rather come here than go to the doctor. Because somehow or another—don't ask me how; don't ask me that because I don't know—but somehow or another God just reaches us and enables us to feel better. And as much as you obey God you can go to God and say, "I obeyed you, Sir, by keeping your faith." Yeah, yeah, that's why we're here.

Members of First Corinthians M.B.C. believe that individuals who are considering joining a church are at a higher risk from the devil because he works harder to bring disaster into their lives to stop them from going with Jesus. As Rev. Thomas puts it, "The devil hates to lose a sinner. He don't like it when it looks like a sinner is going to the other side. When Satan sees someone working hard in the church for the Lord or when he sees someone thinking about joining a church, he gets busy. The devil will try to get to them by bringing some kind of disaster on them."

One of the devil's strategies to undermine the faith of a Christian is to ruin the life of a family member. To make this point, Rev. Thomas offered an example involving a deacon he had met at a convention in 1982. At First Corinthians, a deacon is considered a man whom God has chosen and blessed to serve the church. The congregation expects a deacon and his family to live according to God's precepts and to help others who are seeking God. Thomas told the congregation that while he was at the convention seated next to the deacon and the deacon's wife, they received notice that their son had shot a boy to death in their home. Thomas explained that while the deacon had his mind on the church and was away from home working for the Lord, the devil got to his son. The congregation agreed with his explanation of the deacon's tragedy. Church members consider tragedy a test of an individual's loyalty to God. They believe that God waits to see how someone will respond to disaster just as God waited to see how Jesus would answer to his death on the cross. When faced with tragedy, the congregation recalls Christ's suffering and death and the principles of forgiveness, patience, mercy, and faith embodied in his passion. In their eyes, calamity and ruin are an opportunity for human beings to overcome fear, anger, and frustration.

Joining First Corinthians M.B.C.

Individuals join First Corinthians M.B.C. during worship services when Rev. James Thomas and the assistant ministers open the doors of the church for the invitational call. Prospective new members may come from another church with a letter of reference, or they may enter as candidates for baptism or as Christian witnesses. Before the invitational call, the minister in charge explains the purpose of joining the church. Rev. Thomas made the following statement before the call during one Lord's Supper service:

> Let everyone say amen. We are thankful that the Lord has enabled us to be back again. To each of you who visits here, it is a blessing that God has enabled us just to be here. We haven't done anything to merit this blessing that he has bestowed upon us. But it is because of the grace of God and because of the mercy of God that he has allowed this privilege and opportunity in order to be able to enjoy. I'd like to say to you this evening that if you're not a member of any church, you ought to join a church. If you don't like this church, we will give you a letter to go wherever you want to go. I'd like to point out that if you're not in good fellowship with your own church, you should not be here with us tonight because the Lord has declared that it is damnation to your soul—not only damnation to you but to us who gives it to you. We ask you tonight that if you have not consulted the Lord about the communion, the Lord's Supper that we're now about to take, that you would do so. God is a momentary God, and he does answer prayer right now. He is a prayer-hearing God. What a blessing it is to be under the umbrella of God and to have him saying, "Whoso that will, let him come." I would that you would come this evening if you're not in church. You can come by letter, Christian experience, or candidate for baptism. You just come with us and then go fellowship wherever you so desire. We will send you to any place that you want to go to. But I've come to tell you that he's coming back. I believe he is coming back. He is coming back. And you need to be ready when he comes. You cannot be in the church and out of the church. You cannot be part of the church away from the church. We're asking that you accept him this evening because it is his body that we are part of. He owns us and he expects us to operate by his body.

Among members of First Corinthians M.B.C., it is a blessing for an individual to be at church, where he or she can learn about God's word. Answering the call is the first step toward formally joining the church. A person who answers the call is seeking solidarity with others who believe that Jesus is the way to eternal life. According to church members, while God can lead individuals to the church, he allows them to choose freely between him and the devil. As Rev. Thomas explained, "God can make a way for you to get to church so you can see what it is all about, but God ain't gonna keep you there unless you make up your mind and straighten out your heart to make you want to be there. You have to pray real hard and ask God to hold you because there are a whole lot of other things out there you can get into that are no good for you."

During the invitational call, Rev. Thomas and the congregation sing the invitational hymn, and deacons set up a row of chairs in front of the pulpit facing the congregation; prospective new members come forward and sit in these chairs. Most of the candidates for baptism are children and teenagers who belong to active church families. Rev. Thomas has each candidate for baptism confess that he or she is a sinner and is willing to accept Jesus as savior. He asks them to repeat the following prayer before the congregation: "Lord, I am a sinner, and I want to be saved. I believe you can save me, and I trust you in your word. And I am willing to follow thereafter." Rev. Thomas shakes hands with each candidate after he or she has recited the prayer. He then appoints candidates to the New Members Committee, in which they undergo eight weeks of Christian education in preparation for church membership.

At First Corinthians M.B.C. it is mostly adult women who answer the call as Christian witnesses. The church is elated when males answer the call. Rev. Thomas believes that it is important to get more men involved in the church, and he works on recruiting them. Christian witnesses are people who have been baptized but may not have been active members of a church for some time. Often they are former members of First Corinthians seeking to rededicate themselves to the mission. Church members who miss worship services and Bible classes for over two months without a legitimate excuse are automatically dropped from the church. They may reestablish their membership by answering the call and carrying out their obligations to the church through the New Members Committee.

All adult members of First Corinthians M.B.C. have had a definitive personal experience in which God intervened on their behalf and through which they were converted to the way of God and the church. In church, individuals have opportunities to testify and make their spiritual experiences known to others. They talk about divine intervention in their life when disaster, crises, and affliction strike. In their way of thinking, pain, suffering, and misfortune are a part of divine purpose. In the eyes of church members, the devil, working as God's agent, delivers hardship, sickness, and catastrophe. While testifying, individuals talk about recovering from serious illness; having the strength to endure chronic pain; surviving an assault on the streets; having inadequate food, housing and clothes; dealing with job loss, dissolving marriages, domestic violence, fatal accidents to loved ones, and racial discrimination. They view these hardships as trials that are part of a divine plan to draw people to God and strengthen their faith in him. Rev. Thomas explained the meaning of Christian testimony this way:

> When a person testifies, he tells the disasters that come up on him and how God brought him out through miracle form. We call it being blessed by God that he enabled us to overcome some of the disasters. We believe in some ways that Satan, even though God does not turn us over to him, he still tries to take us in. Many times we get drafted into some kind of obstacles or some of the wrath of Satan, and God has to bring us out because we asked him to do so. Many times it's through our friends, through somebody in our home, through our children. You know, things just come up and we have to get ourselves out. And so we get up and tell one another how it's done, what happens to us and how God blessed. And we call whatever happens to us a blessing, whether its good or bad. We didn't have to have been a bad person for bad things to happen. Things just happen, you know. Many times things that are not well happens to us, and it causes us to turn to him. And we think this is what he really wants us to do; he wants us to be part of his life, a part of his body, a part of his ways. And sometimes we have everything our heart desires, and life is going on, our health is good, and we just proceed to live the way we want to. But then God has a way of cutting us off. And if you don't have everything your heart desires, then you ask him why.

Members of other churches who want to join First Corinthians M.B.C. may present a letter of reference. No one, however, has joined First Corinthians M.B.C. with a letter. Active storefront church members are deeply invested in their churches and rarely depart if all is going well. Typically, congregants leave church because of irreconcilable differences with the church pastor or influential church members. They are bitter when they withdraw and do not ask for their pastor's support to go to another church.

At First Corinthians M.B.C., disaffection and attrition result from competing ambitions for prestigious positions in the church organization. One of the arguments of this study is that viable storefront churches provide working-class blacks with opportunities to gain recognition and spiritual status through their service to the church. Rev. Thomas controls the distribution of volunteer jobs in the church. While he is astute about distributing prestigious positions among church members, there are never enough appointments to accommodate everyone. Problems also arise among members in scrambles for power over church groups. Rev. Thomas must address such disputes, and in doing so, he may alienate ambitious members. Others leave when their personal preferences or circumstances conflict with church doctrines. Rev. Thomas put one man out of the church who was indiscreet with church women and claimed a God-given right to have several wives. Individuals who abuse alcohol and drugs are marginal at First Corinthians. While drugs and alcohol are forbidden, church members are patient with people who use and even abuse them. They believe that alcohol and drug users need spiritual support and that it would be a sin to deny them the help church fellowship offers.

At the end of the invitational call, Laura Watts, the clerk in charge of membership registration, takes the name, address, and phone number of each individual who came forward. She adds the information to the church register and telephones these people during the week. Rev. Thomas appoints them to the New Members Committee and explains their obligations to the church. They must attend eight consecutive weeks of Bible class, Sunday School class, or Wednesday evening prayer services. Individuals who are not baptized qualify for baptism once they have fulfilled these obligations. New members who have been baptized previously are considered regular church members once they discharge their committee obligations. The invitation ends when Rev. James Thomas asks a member seated in the congregation to escort each prospective member back to his or her seat, taking care to match members and candidates in gender and, as closely as possible, in age.

In principle, every member of First Corinthians M.B.C. is an evangelist who is responsible for spreading the word of God. In daily life, church members seize every opportunity to talk with family, friends, and strang-

ers about God and their church. Church members are especially concerned about the spiritual status of their relatives. The majority of the
320 members of First Corinthians M.B.C. are relatives and friends of the
eighteen people who founded the church in 1952.[2] From the day an individual joins First Corinthians, he or she is given a job to do for the church.

Church Organization

First Corinthians M.B.C. is an independent mission supported by resources and volunteer work provided by church members. Rev. James
Thomas and influential church members who joined in the early years
of the mission developed the church organization. None of the individuals who founded First Corinthians M.B.C. and have directed church
affairs are formally trained ministers; they gathered their knowledge of
church administration and organization from their experiences in urban and rural churches before they came together. Many of the conceptual categories and practices at First Corinthians M.B.C. are also found
in other urban black storefront churches (Drake 1940; Drake and Cayton
1945; Williams 1974; Paris 1982). These churches arise from and depend
on the spiritual interests and talents of the people invested in them.

Rev. Thomas and the congregation have established a church organization that accords with their collective spiritual, moral, and social objectives. As has been noted, church members believe God has guided
them and blessed them to establish a church. They believe that God chose
and endowed Rev. Thomas with the personal spiritual qualities to lead
the church, that God reveals plans for the church to him, and that God
expects him to watch over the people and affairs of the church. Church
members also believe that every individual God brings to the church
will be blessed to work in some capacity for the church. They believe
the position that each person will occupy is foreordained. Rev. Thomas
made this point clear during a Baptist Training Union class in which the
assignment was to study the Bible to discern the job of the pastor and
the job of each individual God sends to the church: "Now God doesn't
take folks that ain't right and make them what he wants them to be.
They are that before they are born. Somebody said I heard that old man

---

2. Church members are listed in the bulletin that is passed out each Sunday at church.
During my stay in the field, 320 was the average number of members on the roster.

Riis say God got him out of the gambling shop. Biggest lie that was ever told. Riis was a preacher when he was born. God don't do that kinda business. If you're a preacher now, you was one when you was born. If you're a deacon now, you was one when you was born." Individual predispositions are cultivated in the church through the work of the Holy Spirit. As Diane Carson put it, "The Spirit guides you and gives you a purpose in the church. When you're working with the Spirit, ain't nothing gonna stop you."

Following God's revelations, it is Rev. Thomas's conviction that the interests of First Corinthians M.B.C. are best served by providing a volunteer job in the church for each member and obligating members to accept financial responsibility for the church. For over thirty years, he has directed a church program designed to get congregants invested in First Corinthians M.B.C. by persuading them to contribute their resources and labor to the church. He helps church members come to an understanding of what God wants them to do for the church. In a Baptist Training Union class one Sunday afternoon, Dela Wright explained her view of the role of the pastor in guiding church members to fulfill their spiritual calling: "Rev. James Thomas is our leader. He is a man of God. He is supposed to lead us. We are the sheep. We are to follow him. If he comes to us to tell us something, it is a message from God and we're supposed to do it. Like if he says, 'Sister Wright, I want you to be on this committee, I feel you can do the job.' Reverend already knows. He says, 'Well I think you can do it. God thinks you can do it.' And we should follow him and obey him. He is a man we can trust."

The church organization is divided into committees, boards, and offices.[3] With Rev. Thomas's guidance and support, church members negotiate church vocations. Among active members there is considerable competition for positions in church that confer greater status and power. Individual mobility in the organization depends on gender, age, service, and financial resources. Church members are given an opportunity to work on committees and boards and in offices and thereby gain respectability and status as they fulfill their spiritual aspiration to serve God.

---

3. Until 1982, committees at First Corinthians M.B.C. were called clubs. Rev. James Thomas stopped this practice because, in his view, *club* denotes a secular organization and is therefore inappropriate for the church.

Committees

Rev. James Thomas created the New Members Committee for male and female prospective members who have answered the invitational call. The purpose of the New Members Committee, as he sees it, is to get prospective members involved in the church program, to give them an opportunity to study the word of God, and to impart to them information about church etiquette and routines. Members of the committee are expected to attend eight consecutive weeks of Bible class, Sunday School, or Wednesday evening prayer service before they can join other church groups. Bible study and prayer meetings are considered essential for individual spiritual development. From the start, prospective members must study Scripture for divine inspiration and insight into their purpose at First Corinthians M.B.C.

During their first weeks at First Corinthians, prospective members are on trial; Rev. Thomas and the congregation are examining the seriousness of their intent to serve God. By participating in the routines of the church, new members learn church principles and values that inform individual decorum and enable them to participate meaningfully in church programs. It is important for new members to find a group of people with whom they can establish relations at First Corinthians M.B.C. Church members band with their friends, and new members might feel alone and out of place if it were not for their involvement on the New Members Committee. Members of this committee share the responsibility of meeting new people, learning the practices of the church, and defining a role for themselves at First Corinthians M.B.C. The New Members Committee is a place to make friends, get acquainted with the people and routines of the church, and make contacts that may be useful for moving up in the church organization.

The New Members Committee is the least prestigious at First Corinthians M.B.C. Rev. Thomas has divided this committee into four sections, which are under separate leadership; each section elects a president and a secretary. Thus he has given more ambitious new members an opportunity to gain recognition and enhance their standing in the church. While new members are expected to leave this committee after eight weeks, some stay on it for several months if they are satisfied with the position they have made for themselves. Others remain on the committee until they can manage a move into another group. Newcomers usually leave the church if they do not make friends and establish themselves with a church group.

The Willing Workers Committee includes individuals advancing from the New Members Committee, longtime church members who have a tenuous commitment to the church, and congregants who lack money and ability to raise funds required to take a part in more influential groups. Only women join this committee. Rev. Thomas recruits from among them people to do various tasks such as cleaning the church and cooking church meals. These duties alone offer little by way of recognition and status, but working for Rev. Thomas in church is a way to gain his approval and support. Since the Willing Workers Committee provides little status, congregants avoid it or stay there only for a short period while they work on joining another group. Diligent Willing Workers are viewed favorably at First Corinthians M.B.C. Those members who remain on the committee a long time, however, are marginal in the church; they lack the enthusiasm for church programs that is typical of ambitious members, frequently miss church services, and do not pay their dues. Church members who neglect their accounts, do not attend services regularly, and are not steadily working for the church remain at the lower end of the organization. Willing Workers elect a president and a secretary.

Rev. Thomas established the Beautifying Committee and the Flower Committee to give middle-aged and senior women an honorable way to serve and be recognized in the church. Women on the Beautifying Committee dust the sanctuary weekly and clean and decorate the church for special events. The Flower Committee raises funds to purchase flowers for church programs. The women on these committees have been members of First Corinthians M.B.C. for more than twenty years and have demonstrated loyalty to Rev. Thomas. They consider it a great honor to clean and enhance the appearance of God's house. Among them are women who cleaned the church building when it was an auto repair shop and a glass factory; they proudly talk about the days when they washed the grease off the floor on their hands and knees in the rooms that are now the sanctuary and fellowship hall. The Flower Committee and the Beautifying Committee elect a president and secretary.

The Pastor's Aid Committee is the most prestigious committee for middle-aged and senior women at First Corinthians M.B.C. The women on this committee, appointed by Rev. Thomas, are church members of long standing who have made personal financial contributions to the church, proven their ability to raise church funds, and demonstrated unequivocal loyalty to Thomas. The primary purpose of the Pastor's Aid Committee is to sponsor the pastor's anniversary, a week-long celebration that takes place every year during the second week of May. Committee members' responsibilities include raising funds, planning and coordinating the program for the week, recruiting volunteers to present programs, and getting people to attend the week's events. The pastor's anniversary is one of two major annual fund-raising events at First Corinthians M.B.C. Rev. Thomas also relies on the Pastor's Aid Committee to work for the many ad hoc fund-raising events he sponsors throughout the year. The Pastor's Aid Committee elects a president and a secretary.

Committee Number One is made up of men in their forties and fifties who are also longtime church members and are loyal to Rev. Thomas. They support his church programs with their money and labor. Members of this committee are called trial deacons. They are allowed to attend Deacon Board and Finance Board meetings. They also perform the duties of a deacon during devotional services. Members of Committee Number One enjoy the respect and prestige accorded to church deacons. In the view of the congregation, the Holy Spirit is preparing these men to assume the responsibilities of a deacon. They are expected to keep their mind on the Spirit. They must attend Bible study classes that are conducted for them by Rev. Thomas. Through Bible study, they examine and affirm their commitment to their families and to the church. They also consider their motivation for seeking a position on the Deacon Board. Rev. Thomas decides when a member of Committee Number One is ready to join the Deacon Board. At such time, he and the assistant ministers give a trial deacon an oral examination on the Bible. If he passes the examination, he is crowned during a church ceremony and joins the Deacon Board.

Boards

Service on the Nurses Board offers young and middle-aged women an opportunity to achieve a respectable and praiseworthy position at First Corinthians M.B.C. The Nurses Board is divided into the Senior Board (ages twenty to forty-five) and the Junior Board (ages thirteen to nineteen). Church nurses are expected to work hard, be reliable, and have concern for the well-being of others. Young female church members who appear courteous and responsible and who voluntarily assist church elders and women with small children are encouraged to join the Nurses Board; the qualities these young women embody are viewed in the church as divine gifts needed for service on the board. In addition to demonstrating the appropriate personal qualities for the job, prospective church nurses must pass a first-aid course given at church by Sister Ann Clark, who is a registered nurse.

Nurses are on duty throughout worship services and funerals. During worship services, they dress in uniform: white nylon gown, white cap, white stockings, white orthopedic shoes, and white gloves. While on duty, nurses are alert and ready to help distressed congregants; they carry boxes of tissue and stand by people who need help until they are comforted. Nurses are responsible for protecting congregants who are shouting; a team of nurses makes a circle around a person who is shouting if that person seems likely to harm himself or herself. If the person who is shouting faints, male ushers and deacons will help the nurses get him or her to the lounge for care. Nurses also help women care for their children so that mothers do not have to leave the sanctuary to do so. Nurses carry restless babies and small children from the sanctuary to the lounge, where they change diapers, feed the children, and sit with them. When a restless child settles down, he or she is returned to the mother. First Corinthians M.B.C. members do not believe in keeping infants and children out of the sanctuary during worship services. In their view, the children enhance worship with their innocence, joy, and beauty and the hope they represent for the future. Church members also believe that children must be in the sanctuary during worship to develop their spiritual disposition.

In their roles as church nurses, women achieve respect by demonstrating what the congregation considers prized female attributes: kindness, understanding of children and patience with them, and the will to work hard to help other people. Nurses can increase their status by running for offices on the Nurses Board. The Senior Nurses Board elects a president, a vice-president, and a secretary. The Junior Nurses Board elects a president and secretary: a member of the Senior Nurses Board is elected to supervise the Junior Nurses Board. In addition to their other financial obligations to the church, the nurses pay for their uniforms.

The Usher Board includes men and women divided into senior (ages twenty-five to fifty) and junior (ages thirteen to twenty) groups. For both men and women, serving on the Usher Board is a way to gain respect and recognition in the congregation. The majority of the men on the Usher Board are between the ages of fifteen and thirty-five; most male ushers who make a long-term commitment to the church will seek more influential and prestigious positions available only to men. While women ushers are highly respected at First Corinthians M.B.C., their service on the Usher Board does not help them move into such elevated positions in the organization. A place on the Usher Board is one of the highest-ranking positions women can achieve in the church.

Ushers dress in uniform when they are on duty. Women wear skirts, vests, white shirts, stockings, dress shoes, and white gloves. Men wear white shirts, black ties, three-piece suits, dress shoes, and white gloves. The ushers have three sets of uniforms distinguished by color: white, black, and maroon. White uniforms are worn for funerals and on the first Sunday of every month, which is the day baptism and the Lord's Supper are conducted; for every other occasion the color of the uniform is the president's choice. Members of the Usher Board are on duty during worship services, funerals, weddings, and special programs held in the sanctuary. Throughout these events ushers stand at each entrance to the sanctuary; off-duty ushers sit at the back of the center aisle next to the nurses. While on duty, ushers must be courteous and personable; they are to make everyone who enters the sanctuary feel welcome, and their comportment in church should be exemplary. Ushers seat congregants, hand out bulletins, and follow directions from the deacon and ministers in charge to manage the movement of people in the sanctuary. While ushers are accommodating, they also expect deference from the congregation. Ushers alert nurses when someone in the congregation needs their attention.

Members of the Usher Board may run for Usher Board president, chief, vice-president, and secretary. The Junior Usher Board elects a president and a secretary; a Senior Usher Board member is elected to supervise the Junior Usher Board. The elected offices are especially attractive to female ushers, who wish to increase their influence on the board and to elevate their status in the church. Like the church nurses, ushers pay for their uniforms. Ushers attend weekly meetings led by the president of the Senior Ushers Board.

Storefront church on the West Side of Chicago

Church usher with her children on Sunday morning

Senior church mother on Sunday morning

Church father on Sunday morning

Senior church mothers on Sunday afternoon

Assistant minister (left) and deacons

Junior choir members
on Sunday morning

Church bus driver

Serving the meal after Sunday morning worship

The pastor's table, Sunday dinner

Children playing in front of the church before the afternoon worship service

Visiting minister preaching in front of the church

Junior deacon and his daughter on Sunday morning

Junior Heavenly Knights
at a church reunion in
Alabama

Larson Singers at a church
reunion in Alabama

Mother surrounded by her three children at a church reunion
in Alabama

Mother and her daughters on their way to Sunday worship (photo by Patricia Evans)

Minister preaching on Sunday morning (photo by Patricia Evans)

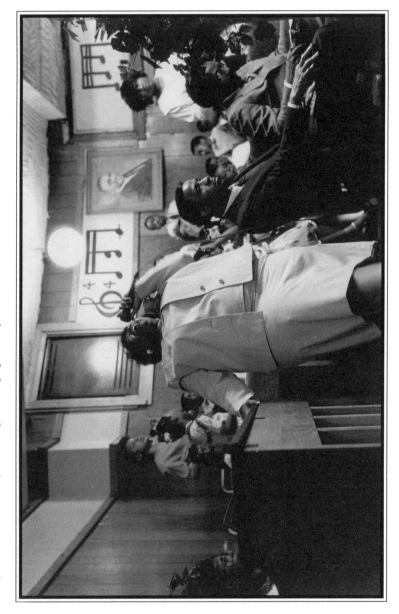

Gospel soloist at Sunday morning worship (photo by Patricia Evans)

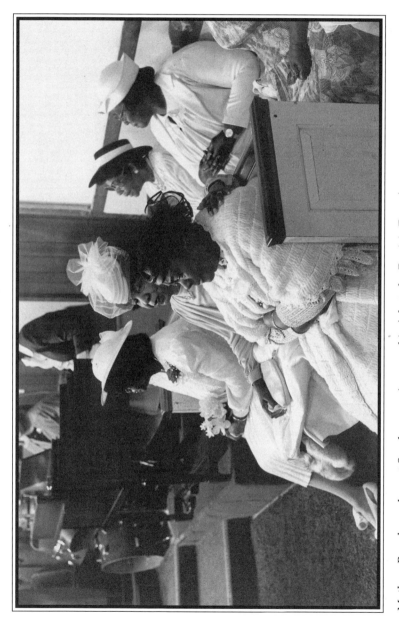

Mothers Board members at Sunday morning worship (photo by Patricia Evans)

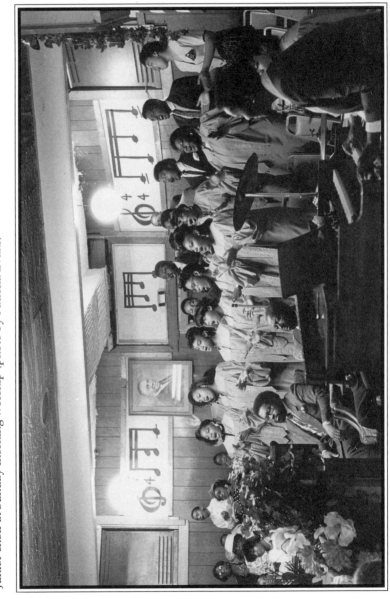

Junior choir at Sunday morning worship (photo by Patricia Evans)

The Mothers Board at First Corinthians M.B.C. is also separated into junior and senior groups; the former includes women between fifty-five and sixty-five; the latter is for women who are over sixty-five. These women are also called church mothers. As church women approach their mid-fifties, they are expected to take their place on the Mothers Board. Some women resist joining the Mothers Board since they must retire from other positions in the organization to do so and thus relinquish influential positions they have cultivated over the years. Other women avoid joining the Mothers Board because they are reluctant to admit their age. Members of the Mothers Board say that through the good and the evil they have known and a lifetime of serving God and their families, they have developed the personal qualities and habit of mind required for service on the Mothers Board. Church mothers are expected to be sober-minded, temperate at all times, and emotionally balanced. They are to avoid calling attention to themselves through their clothing and manners. They are to dress and comport themselves in a reserved and discreet manner. On Sundays they wear white dresses or suits, hats, stockings, and dress shoes. Their outfits represent their spiritual elevation and humility before God. At all times they avoid wearing striking outfits such as those worn by younger women in the church.

It is the duty of church mothers to be moral and spiritual guides to others in the congregation, especially to young women seeking to live in the Spirit. While Rev. Thomas is the moral and spiritual leader of First Corinthians M.B.C. and is available to counsel church members, he believes—as the church members do—that young women would prefer to discuss their personal concerns with other women. Church mothers have the responsibility of counseling younger women. They are women who have been wife to one husband, good mothers and housekeepers, and in the church working for the Lord. The hardships they have endured as wives, mothers, and servants of God are believed to have strengthened them and brought them closer to the Spirit. The church mothers are highly respected and enjoy a great deal of deference from younger women. Church mothers have a significant spiritual role in worship services.

The Deacon Board consists of adult males who have been guided by the Holy Ghost to make a strong commitment to the church. A position on the Deacon Board offers prestige and opportunities to influence the direction of church affairs. Deacons provide a model for other men who seek to live in the Spirit and serve the Lord. They are loyal to Rev. Thomas and have proven their ability to support him in the congregation. Members of the Deacon Board are expected to help their pastor manage the church. The deacons are in charge of church finances; they collect funds raised from tithes and from programs sponsored by church groups. They pay the bills and are also responsible for the maintenance of the church building and the buses. The Deacon Board appoints the church pastor and has the right to ask the pastor to resign. Rev. Thomas relies on deacons to cultivate support for him in the congregation and to discipline congregants who seek to undermine him or the church. Deacons assist Rev. Thomas during worship services and teach Bible classes for adult males. The Deacon Board elects a chairman; B. J. Clark has held this position since 1975. Deacon Clark is committed to Rev. Thomas and follows his advice on church affairs. He addresses the congregation every Sunday morning at the end of the worship service, reiterating the themes presented in Rev. Thomas's sermon and reminding the church members of their financial obligations to the church.

The deacons' spouses sit on the Deaconess Board. A deacon and his wife should grow spiritually and make a firm commitment to the church alongside each other. Like their husbands, deaconesses are moral, spiritual, and social models for others in the church. They are obligated to help the church mothers launder the sacred church linen, which includes the tablecloth used for the Lord's Supper service, baptismal gowns, and seat covers marking the nurses' stations in the sanctuary. For special church programs like the pastor's anniversary and the church anniversary, a deaconess serves as the mistress of ceremonies. On these occasions deaconesses wear tea-length silk or chiffon dresses. For regular church services they wear modest suits and dresses. They may not wear outfits that would be considered flashy or provocative.

The Office of the Assistant Ministers

The Office of the Assistant Ministers includes men called by God to the ministry. With the exception of Rev. Timothy Willis, who was called in his late teens, the assistant ministers were called in their late thirties and forties. These men had been members of First Corinthians M.B.C. for years before they were ordained; their God-given ability to minister was revealed to the church community through their church service. Among the assistant ministers are men who helped establish the church. By way of their spiritual gifts, the assistant ministers help Rev. Thomas lead the church and create the routines and ideas enacted at First Corinthians M.B.C.

Assistant ministers help Rev. Thomas conduct worship services, baptisms, weddings, funerals, the Lord's Supper service, church-wide Bible study, and midweek prayer meetings. When Rev. Thomas is going to be away from the church, he appoints an assistant minister to lead worship services and run the office of the pastor. Assistant ministers also teach Bible classes. In church, they wear three-piece suits. For services, they sit behind the pulpit in a semicircle surrounding Rev. Thomas. Besides him, they are the only ones who may address the congregation from the pulpit.

The Office of the Pastor

As pastor of First Corinthians M.B.C., Rev. James Thomas articulates and teaches God's word for humanity's salvation. In the eyes of his church, God chose him and blessed him to pastor the church. For the first five years he was in charge of First Corinthians M.B.C., he continued to load trucks for a living; since then, he has lived on the salary he earns from the congregation. Throughout the week he is available to anyone in need of counseling for personal problems, marital and family discord, and financial hardship. He spends weekdays visiting the sick in hospitals and homes. He ministers to imprisoned congregants and their incarcerated relatives; he also helps collect funds to bail them out of prison. Rev. Thomas is respected and praised for the comfort he gives to the dying and their families. He helps families plan for funerals. There are no costs to church members for the use of the church for funerals.

It is Rev. Thomas's duty to bring God's word to the congregation through Bible study and worship. Delivering inspiring sermons is one of his principal duties. Congregants hope that, through his preaching, the Holy Spirit will touch them. From his sermons they seek a message from God about their troubles, hoping that God will acknowledge their misfortunes and lift their burden. Rev. Thomas has firsthand knowledge of the daily troubles of church members. He understands the indignity they suffer because they are poor and black. He understands what it feels like to do hard labor and not earn enough for basic provisions. He is concerned about the hungry and homeless who roam the ghetto streets. With parents, he shares the fear of losing a child to drugs, crime, and gangs. He knows what it means to be hungry, jobless, and in a place where nobody knows your name. The congregation views him as a man who, by the grace of God, has endured life's hardships and risen to high office. At First Corinthians M.B.C. he is considered an authority on the Bible, and his church members look to his judgment on interpretation of Scripture. He invokes Scripture in worship service and prayer meetings to help people make sense of the good and bad that comes upon them.

At First Corinthians, Rev. Thomas is considered a person whom God chose to help people understand their purpose in God's mission for their salvation. Thomas told the following story to explain God's reasons for creating the pastor's office:

> A boy that's seventeen years old he said to his daddy, "Today I'm going to let you rest. And I'm going to do all the chores. . . . I'm going to do everything." So he did. Slopped the hogs and fed the mules and fed the cows and goats and everything and got everything ready. You know—like B. J. [Deacon Clark] used to do. He got some smog wood they call kindling in the night wood and he put all that on the porch but then found out all night you got to have a back log. Went out there and he got that back log and he rolled it up to the porch [but] he couldn't get it up there. He got a stick and it fell off the stick. He couldn't get it up there. He just stayed so long until his daddy came to him out on the porch and he said, "Son, is you going to be able to make it?" He said, "I don't think so. I've tried everything. I done all that could be done. I thought I was going to give you a chance to rest tonight." The father said, "Did you try everything?" He said, "Yeah." "Son, I don't think you did." Son said, "Man, don't tell me that. I done everything. I tried everything. I just ain't got the strength to put it up there. There ain't nothing else I could have done." The father said, "You could of asked me to help you."
>
> You see, if you knew what the church is all about, God would be foolish to have me. You don't know. There is no way for you to find out unless God wants it. I don't care how good you can read and what seminary you've been to. You don't know what God has for you. And that's all I'm trying to get us to see.

Throughout the week Rev. Thomas meets with church deacons, assistant ministers, and congregants to plan the church program. Church activities have expanded considerably under his leadership; he expends much energy supervising the program and recruiting volunteers to sustain it. On Tuesday evenings and Sunday mornings he offers Bible classes for church deacons and assistant ministers. He holds Bible class for the entire church every other Sunday afternoon following the church meal.

He also maintains contacts with other storefront congregations. He is the founder and president of the Friendship District, an organization that includes eighteen other storefront ministers. The Friendship District ministers serve as visiting preachers for other churches in the organization, dispatch their church choirs among the other churches to help them celebrate important church anniversaries, and share resources like church buses and facilities. Every July Rev. Thomas returns to Mississippi to conduct revivals at the church where he was baptized and of which he is still a member.

The Mission Circle

Every member of First Corinthians M.B.C. is part of the Mission Circle led by Rev. James Thomas. Thomas divided the Mission Circle into seven groups according to age and gender. Girls and boys between the ages of six and twelve belong to the Girl's Association and the Shepherd Boys. Church members between thirteen and twenty-four are appointed to the Youth Department, which is divided into male and female groups. All males in the church over twenty-four belong to the Brotherhood. Females between twenty-four and thirty-five join the Senior Women Number Two; those who are over forty-five are part of Senior Women Number One.

The primary purpose of the Mission Circle is to provide Christian education for church members. Classes for each group in the Mission Circle are held every Tuesday evening and at least twice a month on Sunday afternoons. Mission Circle Bible study focuses on Christian deportment in church and in the world. Rev. Thomas assigns to each class a Bible teacher and an assistant. In the second week of November, each class elects a president, vice-president, secretary, treasurer, recording secretary, corresponding secretary, financial secretary, and chaplain. Rev. Thomas elects three women from Senior Women Number One to be mission supervisors, each overseeing the activities of the Youth Department, the Junior Women, or the Senior Women Number Two.

Church Choirs

There are four choirs at First Corinthians M.B.C.; the Gospel Choir, the Inspirational Choir, the Youth Angelic Choir, and the Junior Choir. The opportunity to participate in church choirs is prized. The Gospel

Choir is the most prestigious. Members of the Gospel Choir are believed to embody an elevated spiritual status. They are viewed as individuals who communicate with the Holy Spirit through their singing and receive divine messages to enhance the spiritual development of others. Anyone over thirty-five who feels called may audition for the Gospel Choir. Men and women between eighteen and thirty-five may join the Inspirational Choir if the Spirit moves them to sing in the church. Unwed mothers may join the Inspirational Choir but cannot sing with the Gospel Choir.

All of the children in the church between three and twelve belong to the Junior Choir; there are approximately fifty children in this choir. Rev. James Thomas has appointed four adults to supervise the activities of the Junior Choir. He created the Junior Choir and makes the children join it to give them a way to serve the church and learn about God. He also believes that parents are uplifted and feel better about the church and themselves when they see the children praising God.

The Youth Angelic Choir includes males and females between thirteen and seventeen. When they reach the age of twelve, young people must leave the Junior Choir and serve on the Usher Board or the Nurses Board until their thirteenth birthday, when they must decide if they want to stay on the Board or join the Youth Angelic Choir. Unwed teenage mothers and pregnant teens who want to sing in the church cannot join this choir; when they reach eighteen, they have the option of joining the Inspirational Choir.

Each choir elects a president, vice-president, secretary, and treasurer. The Gospel, Inspiration, and Youth Angelic choirs meet every Thursday at 7:00 P.M. in the sanctuary for a short business meeting, Bible class, and rehearsal; Rev. Thomas appoints their Bible teacher from a member of the Gospel Choir. The Junior Choir meets at noon on Saturdays. Junior Choir supervisors conduct a fifteen-minute Bible class with choir members before they rehearse. Several Saturdays during the year the Junior Choir takes field trips. All choir members except those in the Junior Choir must wear their robes when they perform in the church. Because the cost of having children dress in robes every week is prohibitive, Junior Choir members wear robes only for special occasions, like their anniversary and the pastor's and church's anniversary celebrations. The children dress every Sunday according to a color theme selected by their supervisors; pink and white, red and black, yellow and green, and yellow and black are popular color schemes for the children's Sunday outfits.

All of the choirs sing during the Sunday morning service; the Gospel, Inspirational, and Youth Angelic choirs sit on the stage behind Rev. Thomas and the assistant ministers. The Junior Choir sits with its supervisors in the pews near the wall on the left side of the sanctuary. Every fifth Sunday of the month is Youth Day at the church. On that day, the Junior Choir takes the place of the other choirs on the stage. The Gospel, Inspirational, and Youth Angelic choirs also sing during the Lord's Supper service and for funerals. They have several recitals during the year at First Corinthians M.B.C., and they frequently sing as guests in other churches.

Church Finances

Church members recall many financial hard times throughout the history of First Corinthians M.B.C. when they feared they would have to close the church. According to them, God has a plan to finance the church that he revealed to Rev. James Thomas and other church leaders. Rev. Thomas says that whenever the church is in financial trouble, he waits for God to show him what to do.

Members of First Corinthians M.B.C. believe that all things in the universe belong to God and that everything human beings have comes from God. Rev. Thomas explained: "Everything you got, God gives it to you. If you got a job, God give you that job. If you got money, God made that money for you. If you got a place to live, food to eat, nice clothes, and a car, God give it to you. If you got a wife, a husband, a friend, you didn't get it 'cause of anything you did; God give them to you. And God can take it from you just like that." In this cosmos God is in charge of individual social and economic welfare. God dispenses spiritual and material resources among human beings for divine purpose. God gives and takes away material comforts to strengthen individual commitment to the principles of Christian living. God expects individuals to show love for him and for humanity by giving a portion of their God-given labor, money, and talents back to him through the church. Church members believe that in order to receive God's blessings, an individual must approach God with a pure heart. In First Corinthians M.B.C. discourse, the heart is represented in opposition to the mind. Church members say that the mind can make an individual think about doing something for the church, but the thought has to go through the heart for God to receive it. In this cosmology the human capacity for love and faith are generated by the heart. To serve God, individuals must balance ideas and volition generated by the mind with love, faith, and humility from the heart.

Church members believe that God answers the prayers of an individual who prays with a heart that has been converted and is filled with desire to praise and please God. In their vision, however, doubt and disobedience close the channel from the mind to the heart and prevent human beings from receiving God's power and abundance. Although there is ample evidence of God's power to dispense provisions, human beings fail to believe and trust God. According to church members, the devil—the agent of evil in this cosmos—undermines humanity's faith and stops individuals from asking God for his care and provisions. During Bible study, teachers often direct attention to the problem of faith in God. Angela Williams, the teacher of the Junior Women's Bible study group, offered the following biblical example for class discussion on the subject of faith:

> This gospel was written by John, who was a disciple of Christ. We find in the sixth chapter that Christ is among his disciples, and there is something going on. This is a verse that will tell you about the five thousand that he fed. And he spoke to his disciples and he told them to get enough food. As he looked around, there was a multitude coming up. And he went to his disciples and he said, "You go prepare. We have enough money to feed the people." And the disciples state how much money it will cost to feed all these people. And he says, "There is a little boy down below with five barley loaves"—which is like loaves of bread—"and two fish." And Christ said, "We'll sit the people down." And he had them to come to order, and he sat them down. And we find in the Word that Christ took the five loaves from the young man and just began to break it, and before he broke the bread he asked God to bless it and to multiply it for him. And in doing so he took five loaves of bread and two fish and fed five thousand people. Not only did he feed them, but he told the disciples when they finished eating—and people just ate like they wanted to—to pick up whatever is left because he did not want to waste it. And they picked up twelve baskets left from what five thousand men had ate from five loaves of bread and two fish.
>
> But yet we're hungry. Yet we can't trust God enough to feed us. Hallelujah! To supply our need. And this is what our lesson is coming to us. We find that the Lord is letting us know through him what can take place. He can supply what we need. The disciples questioned this. Oh, they marveled at it and asked him how he was able to do this.

The place of faith in God as it determines an individual's ability to give to the church, as members of First Corinthians M.B.C. understand it, became clearer to me in 1984. That year, Rev. Thomas and church deacons launched a fund drive to build a new church. They asked adult members to pledge two hundred dollars for the building fund. In July 1984, I went to visit Rev. Thomas and Deacon B. J. Clark after the Sunday meal. We were seated in the fellowship hall at the pastor's table. Deacon Clark asked me if I would make a two-hundred-dollar pledge for the building fund. This was the first time in three years I had been approached to give money to the church. From the time I started attending worship services, Bible classes, and programs, I made a contribution according to the church schedule. That afternoon I made a two-hundred-dollar pledge but explained that it would take me several months to pay it because I did not have a job. I also told them that I had an interview on the coming Tuesday for a position to teach an anthropology class at Lake Forest College in the fall and that, if I got it, I would be able to give some money toward my pledge. Both men thoughtfully listened to me explain my situation. After some reflection on the matter, Deacon Clark said,

> Well, let me tell you how it works, Francine. We're not going to worry about how you're going to pay; the Lord will handle that. All you have to do is to want to give it from your heart. When it's in your heart to do something or give something to the church, God will bless you so you will do it. Like when I can see we need something in the church, I just keep my mind on the Lord, and the next thing you know, I gets some overtime at work. When I wasn't even expecting it, there be more time I can put on the job and make the money to do what I want to do for the church. Francine, you got to believe and you have to really want to do it for God, and he will take care of it for you.

Rev. Thomas elaborated:

> It's what's in your heart. That's what God looks at. When God looks at your heart and he can see you want to do something for him in the church, he will open the door. I can tell you about some days where we didn't know next week how we were gonna keep the lights on and the heat on in the church. The first service we ever had in this place when we had just rented here, Brother Clark, myself, and some others you've been knowing in the church put their little money in and we worked day and night. And we prayed;

yes, we prayed. There was a whole lot of things we needed, and we didn't have them, and we didn't know where we was gonna get them. But we just believed that God would help us. The first service we had on a Sunday, we stayed up all night, and we worked it just to get ready for service. Come morning we had service. We all stood in a circle holding hands and prayed. We didn't lift an offering. Somehow or another I just didn't think it was right to take up a collection. We prayed and we went home to rest. We didn't know how we would make it right then, but the Lord just kept blessing; he just kept blessing. And we never did stop believing in what he could do. I just knew he would keep putting it in people's hearts to give and do for the church. And he has been blessing us ever since. And that's what you have to do. You have to make up your mind and get it in your heart that you want to do it for God. Then keep your trust in God and leave it alone.

On Tuesday I met with the anthropology department chairman and dean at Lake Forest College. Before my interview with the dean, the chairman told me the salary they were offering. During my meeting with the dean we did not discuss the salary. That evening, the chairman called me and said, "Frances, good news: the position is yours. The dean seemed to like you. We would like to offer you the position, and the dean said to increase your salary another two hundred dollars." I accepted the offer. I was astonished by the unexpected salary increase, which matched my pledge to the church. The following Sunday, I found Deacon Clark and Rev. Thomas at their table in the fellowship hall and told them what had happened. They were amused but not surprised. Rev. Thomas said, "Yeah, that's what the Lord will do. When you don't expect it, he will put it in your hands." The following Sunday, Rev. Thomas included my experience in his sermon, and he often recalls it as an example for others when I am back in church.

Church members learn about their financial obligations to the church by reflecting on Scriptures presented during worship services and Bible classes and in church bulletins. The following Scriptures, with their related headings, are printed in the bulletin distributed every Sunday morning during the worship service. They sum up the collective disposition of the congregation on supporting the church.

GOD CLAIMS A PORTION OF OUR SUBSTANCE: And all the Tithes of the Land, whether of the seed of the land, or of the fruit of the tree, is the Lord's: It is Holy unto the Lord.

WITHHOLDING THIS CLAIM IS TO ROB GOD: Will a man rob God? Yet ye have robbed me. But ye say, wherein have we robbed thee? In Tithes and Offerings.

THEREFORE THE CLAIM SHOULD BE ATTENDED PROMPTLY: And as soon as the Commandment came abroad, the children of Israel brought in abundance the first fruits of corn, wine, oil, and honey, and all of the increase of the field; and the Tithes of all the things brought they in abundantly.

WORLDLY PROSPERITY PROMISED TO THOSE WHO HONOR GOD WITH THEIR SUBSTANCE: Honor the Lord with thy substance, and with the first fruits of all thine increase; so shall thy barns be filled with plenty, and thy presses shall burst with new wine.

IT SHOULD BE GIVEN WILLINGLY: Every man according as the purpose in his heart, so let him give; not grudgingly, or of necessity, for God loveth a cheerful giver.

DOES POVERTY OR LIMITED MEANS EXCUSE ANY ONE FROM GIVING TO THE LORD: They shall not appear before the Lord empty: EVERY MAN SHALL GIVE as he is able, according to the blessing of the Lord thy God which he hath given thee. And none shall appear before me empty.

GIVE THAT SOMETHING EVERY SUNDAY: Upon the first day of the week.

ACCORDING TO THE BLESSINGS RECEIVED: According as the Lord thy God hath blessed thee.

Bible study groups discuss these and other biblical sources to give meaning to work and money. In Bible study, individuals discuss the meaning of changing material fortunes and what it means to them to give resources to the church. Funds for the church are collected according to a schedule established by Rev. Thomas and church deacons. On Sunday, every member is expected to tithe. Ten percent of an individual's weekly income is considered, as the Sunday bulletin states, "something you owe God." In the bulletin the name of each church member is listed under the group he or she belongs to. Next to each name appears the amount of that person's contribution for each week through the month; bulletins are updated every week.

For the privilege of membership in a church group, individuals pay dues once a year when the group celebrates its Annual Day. These assessments have been from thirty-five to fifty dollars; fees are higher for members of more prestigious groups like the Gospel Choir and the Deacon Board. There are several occasions during the year when they are expected to pay dues. See Table 1 for Annual Day assessments and Table 2 for membership tithes.

Table 1
ANNUAL DAY ASSESSMENTS ($)

	Men	Women	Working Young Adults	Non–Working Young Adults	Children
Winter Harvest Tea	20	20	7	5	2
Men's Day	50	25	15	10	2
Women's Day	25	35	15	5	2
Pastor's Anniversary	65	65	20	15	5
Mission Day	10	10	5	3	1
Building Fund Service	50	50	15	10	2
State Tea	35	35	25	7	5
Church Anniversary	100	100	25	20	5
Special Classes	36	36	21	21	6
Total	391	376	148	96	30

NOTES: Children are expected to begin paying assessment at the age of five.
Young adults are church members between the ages of 13 and 19.
Special classes are held on an ad hoc basis during the year.

Throughout the week, money is collected from Sunday School classes, Bible study classes, evening prayer meeting, and weeknight worship services; adults pay a dollar and teens and children give twenty-five to fifty cents. Several times a year, special Christian education classes and revivals are sponsored at First Corinthians M.B.C. Fees for these programs are thirty-six dollars for adult men and women, twenty-one dollars for working teenagers, twenty-one dollars for nonworking members, and six dollars for children.

Members of First Corinthians M.B.C. are either unemployed, on welfare, or in low-paying jobs; only a few have had steady work providing a good hourly wage. Thus for the majority of members in this church, complete payment of church subscriptions would be prohibitive. Most members make partial payments to their various church accounts to maintain their standing in the church at large and among their church peers. On Sunday, only half of the members listed in the bulletin tithe. Those who default because of extreme poverty or are undergoing severe hardship are not ostracized. Personal misfortune is considered part of a divine plan to build trust in God and must be endured through the church. The church, on the other hand, will not tolerate individuals who neglect their dues while flaunting personal acquisitions like extravagant automobiles or clothes. In this cosmos God and his people are unimpressed by individuals who do not use their material possessions to benefit the church.

Table: 2
MEMBERSHIP TITHES

	1984	1985	1986
Deacon Board	730.21	725.52	754.50
Deaconess Board	231.00	310.00	160.00
Ministers Board	323.00	839.00	643.04
Mothers Board	342.00	813.00	462.10
Beautifying Committee	274.56	347.25	449.40
Willing Workers Committee	204.80	947.74	726.00
Pastor's Aid Committee	133.00	149.00	116.00
Flower Committee	350.00	393.20	401.70
Senior Nurses Board	202.50	329.57	339.50
Senior Usher Board	540.63	771.50	1,115.00
Committee One	426.77	1,083.60	1,106.11
Inspirational Choir	452.15	719.50	1,018.69
Gospel Choir	692.99	987.43	1,066.16
Young Adult Choir	412.27	505.08	529.78
Junior Choir	120.85	260.75	234.07
New Members Committee One	370.00	319.00	210.00
New Members Committee Two	18.00	106.00	239.00
New Members Committee Three	415.00	172.00	242.00
New Members Committee Four	111.50	442.00	454.00
Junior Nurses Board	63.00	59.50	67.00
Junior Usher Board	53.25	28.00	29.00
Total	6,600.48	10,457.64	10,479.05

In the cosmology of First Corinthians, God rules over humanity's fortunes and misfortunes. Work, wages, welfare, joblessness, and destitution are part of his plan to conquer evil and save humanity. According to church members, human beings labor in God's vineyard, and the harvest belongs to God. In this worldview money and the things it can buy have no moral or social value unless they are offered back to God. Members of First Corinthians M.B.C. believe that money cannot buy God or eternal life. Rev. Thomas explained, "God does not need your money. All the money and nice things in the world can't do nothing for you when it comes time for you to die if God isn't with you." The privileges of money are subverted by the certainty of death and the hope for eternal life, which is possible through the will of God and service to him and humanity through the church.

The Church Building

First Corinthians M.B.C. stands amid a game room, a transient hotel, a hand car wash, a tire repair shop, and an unpaved parking lot in Garfield Park. The church is located in a rickety building abandoned during the race riots in the late 1960s. Several buildings surrounding First Corinthians M.B.C. were burned, looted, and abandoned in the rioting and have not been rehabilitated. The present church quarters were two adjacent storefronts; one was an automobile mechanics shop, the other a small-scale glass factory. Rev. James Thomas said that in 1965 the Holy Spirit guided him to move the congregation into the abandoned mechanics shop; two years later they rented the glass factory. First Corinthians M.B.C. was established in 1950 and moved four times before the congregation occupied the present quarters, where the church has been since 1965.

Rev. Thomas explained that the church's founders created the church in their image of God's house in heaven and according to their understanding of God's principles governing individual and collective deportment in the church. The group prayed and invoked the Holy Spirit for supplies and labor to build the church. Rev. Thomas, Deacon Clark, and other members remember working all night long to get the space ready for the first church service and going straight to their jobs following morning worship. Senior church women still talk about cleaning the grease off the floors on their hands and knees. The furnishings in the church were bought in used furniture shops and flee markets and collected from rubbish dumps. The church pews were purchased in 1965 from a failed storefront church.

When the congregation rented the storefront, the building's room was oblong, with exposed red brick interior walls and cement floors. There are no windows on the building. Shopkeepers on this street have replaced glass windows with red and yellow bricks. In the center of the building's yellow-brick facade there is a large gray metal door. Above the door is a sign bearing the name of the church and pastor. Above that sign there is a white concrete cross. To the right of the doors there are three rectangular wooden frames enclosing colored plastic that looks like stained glass; the frames are mounted on the brick wall. To the left of the door, the church schedule is posted on the wall in a glass frame; the glass has been broken since I started going to the church.

In the sanctuary there are thirty-one rows of wooden pews in the center aisles and ten rows along the walls on each side. Nurses' stations are marked by a white satin cloth with a red cross. The stations are in the front, middle, and back rows of the center aisle. The interior brick walls are covered with assorted wooden panels. In the back of the sanctuary, there are two doors leading to aisles that extend to the front, where there is a stage. A wooden pulpit stands center-stage. Varied upholstered chairs are arranged in a semicircle behind the pulpit; these seats are reserved for the pastor, assistant ministers, and guest ministers. Behind the row of chairs, assorted folding chairs and wooden benches are arranged in tiers for the choir. On the stage to the left of the pulpit, near the wall, there are drums and an organ; to the right, there is a piano. On the wall behind the piano there is a round black-and-white clock. Microphones are set on the pulpit and on the stage to the right and left of the pulpit. Loudspeakers are attached to the walls of the sanctuary a few feet below the ceiling. The deacons and women address the congregation from these microphones. A United States flag is set near the organ. The stage is decorated with an assortment of colorful plastic flowers and plastic foliage. The sanctuary is used for worship services, prayer meetings, Bible classes, funerals, weddings, choir rehearsals, and business meetings.

On the floor space in front of the stage, the congregation constructed a cement pool six feet long, five feet wide, and four feet deep. The pool is used for the Baptism service, which is held every first Sunday of the month at 5:00 P.M. The rest of the time, the pool is covered by wooden boards and a piece of red carpet. Over the covered pool are an offering table and two wooden chairs. For the Lord's Supper service, held every first Sunday evening of the month after the Baptism service, another table called the Lord's Supper table is used instead of the offering table. Church members consider the Lord's Supper table highly sacred. Only the deacons, ministers, and members of the Mothers Board are allowed to handle it. Above the pulpit there is a white banner bearing the church's name, the pastor's name, and the church theme: "Be not deceived for

God is not mocked; whatever a man soweth, that shall he also reap"
(Gal. 6:7). Rev. Thomas selected this Scripture for the church theme in
1967, and it is printed on the first page of all church bulletins. On the
wall behind the stage there is a black-and-white portrait of Thomas taken
shortly after he was elected pastor.

Above the entrance to the sanctuary, the church founders constructed
a loft that is divided into two rooms: one serves as the pastor's office,
and the other is the church clerk's office. The pastor's office contains a
large wooden desk and a black chair, two upholstered chairs, a small
cot, a small bookcase, and a coatrack. Behind the desk there is a glass-
covered wooden bookcase that holds a 1972 edition of *The World Book
Encyclopedia*. On top of the bookcase there are several trophies that the
Heavenly Knights won over the years. On the wall opposite the desk
there is a map displaying the kings and queens of Africa. The clerk's
office contains a small desk and chair, file cabinet, manual typewriter,
and mimeograph machine. There are telephones in each office. There is
also a telephone on the stage in the sanctuary and a public phone in the
fellowship hall. The pastor, assistant ministers, and deacons use the loft
for their meetings.

On the right side of the sanctuary, near the stage, there is a door leading to the fellowship hall. The church covenant is mounted above this
door. Rev. Thomas discovered the church covenant in some literature
he received at a Baptist convention in the mid-1960s; he could not iden-
tify the exact source. He believes that the covenant summarizes the values of the church and the way Christians must conduct themselves in
the world and that it is important for church members to read, study,
and discuss it often. It is hand-written with a black marker on a white
poster. It states:

> Having been led, as we believe by the Spirit of God, to receive the Lord
> Jesus Christ as our Savior and, on the profession of our faith, having been
> baptized in the name of the Father, and the Son, and of the Holy Ghost, we
> do now, in the presence of God, and this assembly, most solemnly and joy-
> fully enter into covenant with one another as one body in Christ. We engage,
> therefore, by the aid of the Holy Spirit to walk together in Christian love; to
> strive for the advancement of this church, in knowledge, holiness, and com-
> fort; to promote its prosperity and spirituality to sustain its worship, ordi-
> nances, discipline, and doctrines to contribute cheerfully and regularly to
> the support of the Ministry, the expenses of the church, the relief of the poor,
> and the spread of the gospel through all nations. We also engage to maintain

family and secret devotion; to religiously educate our children; to seek the salvation of our kindred and acquaintances; to walk circumspectly in the world; to be just in our dealings, faithful in our engagements, and exemplary in our Department; to avoid all tattling, backbiting, and excessive anger; to abstain from the sale of and use of intoxicating drinks as a beverage; to be zealous in our efforts to advance the kingdom of our Savior. We further engage to watch over one another in brotherly love; to remember one another in prayer; to aid one another in sickness and distress; to cultivate Christian sympathy in feelings and Christian courtesy in speech; to be slow to take offense, but always ready for reconciliation and mindful of the rules of our Savior to secure it without delay. We moreover engage that when we remove from this place, we will soon as possible unite with some other church where we can carry out the spirit of the covenant and the principles of God's word.

The covenant is also printed in the back page of the Sunday bulletin. Rev. Thomas and Bible study leaders refer to the covenant often in Bible classes.

The walls of the fellowship hall are covered with assorted wood panels. There are two rows of rectangular tables with chairs, ten on each side. At the back of this room there are two gray metal desks. A black couch, recovered from an alley in 1985, has been placed on a wooden platform near the desks. There are two steam tables and a counter near a door that leads to the kitchen. There is a window in the wall that separates the kitchen from the fellowship hall through which food and messages are passed during church meals. The kitchen is furnished with appliances acquired from a restaurant that failed. These rooms are used for meetings, classes, fund-raising events, church meals, weddings, and funerals.

The church has two lounges; one is off the sanctuary, the other behind the kitchen. The lounge near the sanctuary is equipped with a crib, a cot, a full-length mirror, a table, and chairs. Members of the Nurses Board use this lounge to care for infants and for congregants who are overwhelmed during church services. The other lounge has two large sofas, a wooden desk, and chairs. The senior mothers go to this lounge when they want to escape the hustle and bustle of the fellowship hall. Church members use both lounges to change into their church uniforms and outfits. Sunday School and Bible classes also meet in the lounges.

Smoking, drinking alcoholic beverages, chewing gum, and running are prohibited in the church. Members who smoke walk several feet away from the church building entrance before lighting cigarettes. Young adults do not smoke near the church or in the presence of church members. Food and beverages can be taken only in the fellowship hall, though infants are bottle-fed in the sanctuary. Unnecessary conversation in the sanctuary is not allowed. Women cannot wear slacks on the church premises at any time. The following church rules for better service are posted in the corridor leading to the sanctuary and printed every Sunday in the church bulletin:

> 1. Please don't walk when the Minister is Speaking, when Prayer is being offered, Scripture Reading, Welcome Address, Announcements, Extending of Invitation, Choirs Singing Solos and hymns.
>
> 2. The house of God is a "Holy Place." Let us "Not" visit in service. You could hinder a Blessing.
>
> 3. Please obey the rules of Ushering for Better Service.
>
> 4. We are asking all Mothers to please instruct your children not to run or play in the Church, or talk, Chew Gum, or eat candy in Service. "This is a Holy Place."
>
> 5. No Gum Chewing or Talking in Service.
>
> 6. Parents, please encourage your children to attend Sunday School, Bible Class for the betterment of the church.
>
> 7. We have been asking all children out of the Fellowship Hall while Service is in progress. Parents, Please instruct your children to do so, likewise, you do the same.
>
> 8. Let us not destroy what we have, but Pray for an increase in what we need ("God's Power").

These rules are strictly enforced by church ushers and officers; there are seldom any serious infractions.

The sidewalk in front of the church is a place to socialize. On warm days, church members gather there and visit with friends going to and coming from church services. The sidewalk is especially busy on Sunday afternoon and evening. Children play and walk to the corner grocer or to the ice cream truck parked near the church to buy snacks with nickels and dimes they collect from relatives and family friends. The sidewalk is a spot for small talk and private conversation. People gather with their Bibles to discuss Scripture and testify; a marginal visiting preacher may seize the opportunity to preach. For some, the sidewalk is a place to relax between services. It is also the locus for courtship, flirtations, and bantering.

Rev. James Thomas parks his black Fleetwood Cadillac—a gift from the congregation in 1981 for his sixteenth anniversary as church pastor—in front of the church entrance; no one else takes that space. There is a fire hydrant where he parks, but he never gets a parking ticket. Church members park their cars as close to the church as possible to avoid having them stolen; during church services, men take turns watching cars that belong to church members. Between services on Sunday, church members sit and visit in their cars. They consider the streets and vacant lots around the church dangerous and stay near the church entrance.

CHAPTER FIVE

Church Activities

At First Corinthians M.B.C. the congregation's interpretation of the biblical story informs and shapes worship services, Bible study, and prayer meetings. Members of First Corinthians do not see themselves as an impoverished and marginal community. In their conception, God empowers Christians to withstand social injustice and oppression. Through Bible study and worship, members of First Corinthians seek spiritual knowledge, which for them is the source of supreme power in the universe. In the narratives members articulate during worship and Bible study, they create a self-determined and principled way of life. In church practices they reach for beauty, dignity, fairness, wisdom, and joy that defy ghetto poverty, exploitation, injustice, and suffering. Through their church, they claim God's promise to reverse the fortunes of oppressed people.

The Lord's Day at
First Corinthians M. B. C.

Sunday is the most active day of the week at First Corinthians M.B.C. Members call it the Lord's Day. According to them, God set Sunday apart from the other days of the week to give good and faithful Christians a day to praise him, learn about him, and work for the salvation of humanity. Sunday is not a day of rest, they say; "Sunday is the hardest day of the week for Christians who know the importance of worship and

---

The interpretive information in this chapter is based on tape-recorded Bible study sessions, sermons, and worship services and on tape-recorded interviews with church members over a three-year period.

Bible study." Sunday programs are scheduled from 9:00 A.M. until 8:30 P.M. Between 8:30 and 9:00 A.M., congregants arrive by public transportation and in car pools. In 1985 the church purchased two used buses for field trips, and there has been discussion about using them to transport members to and from church on Sunday. Since members must be in church early on Sunday, they prepare beforehand; in the households I visited, women bathed children, combed their hair, and washed and ironed clothes for church throughout the evening on Saturday so that everyone would be ready for church on time the next morning.

On Sunday morning members greet each other warmly, shaking hands and engaging in small talk before they enter the sanctuary. There are joy and excitement in the air as people gather. One Sunday morning a senior mother greeted her friends in the fellowship hall with these words: "Lord knows it's a blessing to fellowship. There ain't nothing like coming to this here old church to be with people who know how to treat you right. There ain't nothing like coming here to the house of the Lord to praise God, to be with people you can trust, have some fun, and get your mind off things for a little while." As members arrive, they say, their spirits are uplifted by the thought that God has given them another week to come to church to worship and glorify Him.

It is Rev. James Thomas's goal to have everyone stay in church the entire day on Sunday. He works with church groups to sponsor Sunday activities that will attract church members. The Sunday morning activities include Sunday school and the worship service following it. After the worship service, a dinner is served. There is at least an hour between the end of dinner and the start of the evening program. After dinner people move about and visit. When the weather is good, most of the action takes place on the sidewalk in front of the church. In the spring and summer a truck vendor selling ice cream and cold soda pop parks near the church. Children play outside and visit the truck to buy treats. At the west end of the block there is a small candy store that children visit throughout the afternoon. Adults gather outside the church to get away from the crowd, have a cold drink, and visit with friends. Smoking is not permitted on church grounds. Adults who smoke walk several feet away from the church entrance before lighting a cigarette. During this hour inside and outside the church there is much joking, laughing, courting, and amiable bantering among the crowd. On the first Sunday of every month the evening program includes Baptist Training Union service at 4:30, baptism service at 5:30, and the Lord's Supper service at

7:00. Every other Sunday of the month Rev. Thomas and representatives of church groups schedule Bible classes, short worship services, and gospel music recitals. There are also annual church celebrations (see table 3). At least one Sunday a month, First Corinthians M.B.C. is invited to another church; the church buses are used for these trips. Funerals are held on Sunday nights as well as weeknights at 8:00; on First Sunday, funeral services immediately follow the Lord's Supper.

Table 3
ANNUAL DAYS

Month	Performer
January	Installation Service Winter Harvest Tea
February	Men's Day
March	Building Fund Service
April	Inspirational Choir Anniversary Women's Day
May	Mother's Day Pastor's Anniversary
June	Father's Day Young Adult Choir Anniversary
July	Sunday School and New Members Day Willing Workers, Beautifying, Flower Anniversary State Tea
August	Nurses Board Anniversary Building Fund
September	Gospel Choir Anniversary
October	Usher Board Anniversary Combined Choirs Anniversary
November	Church Anniversary Mission Day

While most members do stay in church all day on Sunday, those who have to work come for part of the day. Church members are distressed when they have to miss church because of work. They negotiate with their bosses and coworkers and trade off holidays and desired day shifts to get Sunday off. When looking for work, they let prospective employers know that they are willing to work all shifts every day except Sunday.

Lenora Johnson is among the deeply committed church members who refuse to work on Sunday. She is in her mid-thirties. She is president of the Junior Women's Mission Circle and sings with the Gospel Choir. Her husband, Rev. Arthur Johnson, is in his early forties and a member of the Assistant Ministers Board. They have four children who are active in the church. Lenora Johnson says she has been coming to First Corinthians M.B.C. since she settled in Chicago. Rev. Charles Larson is her mother's brother, and he brought her family to the church when they moved to the city in 1954; her mother, two sisters, and four brothers are also active members of First Corinthians M.B.C.

In 1985 the factory where Arthur Johnson worked shut down, and he was laid off. He could not find work. Lenora, who had stayed at home since her first child was born, looked for work. Through a church friend she found a job in a suburban nursing home. When she interviewed for the position, she made it clear that she would not work on Sunday because she went to church with her family that day. The supervisor who hired her agreed to the terms. Less than two months into the job, however, the supervisor scheduled her to work on Sunday. At first she managed by changing shifts with other employees who did not mind working on Sunday. When her supervisor scheduled her to work every Sunday, Lenora Johnson explained that anything she would make on Sunday the Lord would take away, and she quit the job. After that she started cooking meals in her kitchen to sell at the factory where her cousin, Jackie Evans's husband, and several other men from the church work. She learned to cook while working in Rev. Frank Dixon's diner as a teenager when she first came to the city. Rev. Johnson helps his wife run the business by delivering the meals to the factory. While they struggled financially, the business out of their kitchen was the best opportunity they had to earn cash. They are not alone in their determination among members of this congregation to find work that does not interfere with church on Sunday.

Sunday School

At First Corinthians M.B.C. there is a great deal of emphasis on learning God's word through Bible study. Firsthand knowledge of Scripture
is considered essential for living according to God's plan. For members
of this congregation, Bible study is a source of spiritual empowerment
to withstand evil, uncertainty, and life's hardships. Angela Williams explained the significance of studying the Bible to her class this way:

> And we come to find out in our lesson that the word of God is the power
> unto salvation. This is our power. This is what Rev. James Thomas was just
> talking about. Without the word you have no power. You don't have any-
> thing to do nothing with. You cannot fight Satan. You cannot sustain yourself
> without knowing the word. Now those of you that are weak in faith, this is
> why you are weak—because you do not have the word of God. Once you
> have the word of God, it will strengthen you. This is where your strength
> comes from. You can pray all night. You will not get strength from prayer.
> The only thing it will do for you is to have the Lord have more mercy on you
> because of the fact that you have enough sense to go to him and ask him to
> do some things for you. But he will not do nothing until you strengthen your-
> self by reading the Bible.

Sunday school is one of three Bible classes offered at First Corinthians
M.B.C.; the others are the Mission Bible classes held on Tuesday evening
and Baptist Training Union classes scheduled at least twice a month on
Sunday evening. At First Corinthians M.B.C. there is much enthusiasm
for Bible study; over half of the congregation attends classes every Sunday.

Deacon Albert Watts has been superintendent of the Sunday School
at First Corinthians M.B.C. since 1969. He joined the congregation in
1954. He was born in West Virginia, where he worked in the coal mines.
His mother, Emma Watts, and his sister, Katina Watts, left West Virginia
in the mid-1940s and settled in Chicago. Deacon Watts and his wife,
Laura, also left West Virginia in the mid-1940s and moved in with Emma
and Katina in Chicago. Albert and Laura Watts married shortly after
they settled in Chicago. One of Emma Watts's coworkers took her to
First Corinthians M.B.C. in 1953, the year that the rest of the family started
attending Sunday services there regularly. Albert and Laura Watts have
been members of First Corinthians ever since. Laura Watts says, "The
church is all the family I got up here besides my husband and them

because I came up here alone with Albert and none of my people came with me."

Deacon Watts is deeply committed to the Sunday school and likes to talk about his accomplishments with the program. He proudly presents himself as the man who has the skills, self-discipline, character, spiritual conviction, and contacts to get the job done. When Watts took over the Sunday School program, there was one class; by the mid-1980s there were thirty-two. A hundred and fifty or so people attend Sunday school classes each week. Deacon Watts believes that one of his most important tasks is getting church members to attend these classes. He is proud of the Christian education program he has developed and firmly believes that participants benefit spiritually from it. Every Sunday he arrives at church by bus with his family before 8:00 A.M., and the family stays in church the entire day. Throughout the day, he concentrates on building the Sunday school program.

Deacon Watts recruits teachers from among church members. He trains them and appoints them to a class. He has thirty-two teachers and ten substitutes. When asked how he selects his teachers, he said,

> You have to know people; you have to know them real good. A teacher always gives more than they get back. You look for somebody who can do that. A teacher has to have patience. They have to be good on patience because their students will never know as much as they do. Students have to see something in a teacher, and the teacher has to see something in them. If they don't, they will never be able to teach them anything. The way to get that kind of a bond is the teacher has to be on time for class, they have to be prepared with the lesson, and they have to know more than the students.

Deacon Watts believes in hard work, punctuality, order, and self-discipline. He demonstrates these qualities in his demeanor and seeks to develop them among his staff and students. He meets with the Sunday school teachers every Saturday afternoon to go over lessons, classroom management, and principles of effective Sunday School teaching. He also believes that people should be rewarded for their work. Once a year he holds an assembly to honor dedicated students and teachers. During the assembly he gives certificates to students and teachers for good attendance and to classes that have given outstanding financial support to the Sunday school. He gives diplomas to students when they advance into a higher grade.

Sunday school begins at 9:00 A.M. with all classes present in the sanctuary. Deacon Watts rings a bell that is on the offering table in front of the pulpit; this signals the start of the session. He leads the assembled classes in a hymn and prayer before they break up to meet separately for forty-five minutes. The sanctuary, fellowship hall, lounges, and offices in the loft are used as classrooms. Deacon Watts has a class for every church member, placing each according to age, gender, and position in the church organization. Classes accommodate ages three to sixty-five and over. Infants and toddlers sit in class with their mothers or older siblings. Deacon Watts believes that good habits and a positive attitude toward Sunday school must be inculcated in small children. He is tolerant with restless infants and youngsters, and he instructs teachers and students to be kind to and patient with them. He believes that it is important for teenagers and young children to learn to take responsibility for the younger children.

The purpose of the Sunday school is to teach the Bible, which at First Corinthians M.B.C. is considered the infallible word of God. Young-adult and adult classes study the Adult Christian Life books published by the National Baptist Publishing Board in Nashville, Tennessee. The books are purchased with funds raised by the Sunday School Board and are given to students. Each week, every class covers the same chapter in the book. In classes for small children the teachers tell a story based on the main thought and Scriptures in the lesson. Teachers give the children crayons and paper to draw pictures about the story. At the start of the class, teachers and students recite the main idea of the lesson. Teachers then call on individual students to read the Scriptures. The reading is followed by a discussion in which students are asked to think about their lives in light of the lesson. Teachers encourage students to discuss the ways in which God is working in their lives and in the world. Toward the end of the session, the class secretary takes attendance and collects a fee from students; adults pay one dollar and children and teens give twenty-five to fifty cents.

All classes meet again in the sanctuary under the direction of Deacon Watts. He asks six teachers to send a student from their classes to the front of the sanctuary. He calls the names of ten small children and has them stand before the congregation with their pictures. The children show their pictures and are encouraged to say a few words about them. He asks each student to explain the meaning of the Scripture in the day's lesson. For children and teens this is a chance to practice addressing the congregation, which Deacon Watts and the Sunday school staff agree is a necessary skill for developing self-esteem and respect in the church. Adults may seize the opportunity to testify. After the students have addressed the congregation, Deacon Watts calls on the class secretaries and treasurers to report attendance and the amount of money collected in their classes that morning. The money is given to the secretary of the Sunday School Board, who is seated next to Deacon Watts at the table in front of the sanctuary. Deacon Watts then briefly discusses the lesson and reminds everyone of the importance of Christian education, after which he turns the classes over to Rev. James Thomas, who always stresses the personal empowerment to be gained through Bible study and knowledge of the Word of God. He praises the group for attending Sunday school. Before he dismisses the classes, he announces the program for that day and urges everyone to attend.

Deacon Watts spends a considerable amount of time creating incentives to get people to attend Sunday school. One of his most successful plans is the coffee hour, which immediately follows Sunday school. After they have been dismissed by Rev. Thomas, congregants leave the sanctuary and enter the fellowship hall, where free coffee and sweet rolls (cut in half so that everyone will get a piece) are served. During the coffee hour friends gather to talk about their week and catch up on the latest news going around the church. They also use this time to promote programs their church groups are sponsoring. Deacon Watts moves about the crowd, personally thanking people who were in class that morning. He asks each person he greets to make a commitment to be in class again next Sunday. He approaches as many people as he can. Individuals who come to the coffee hour without having attended Sunday school avoid Deacon Watts because they know he will reproach them for missing the class.

In everyday life Albert Watts is a custodian in a public grammar school on the West Side of Chicago; he has worked there since the mid-1960s. At school he does not hesitate to discipline children in the halls and on the playground. He says he knows all the children at the school and that they all know him. Watts explained that he does more than mop floors and clean at the public school. By watching how things get done there, he has learned a great deal about managing teachers, students, and classes. He believes that the public schools fail children because there is no respect for teachers or students. He also believes that students and teachers in public school fall short of their aim because they lack purpose and motivation.

Albert and Laura Watts live in a high-rise public housing development located within three miles of the church. They have two children,
Alice and Tyrone. Alice has five children. She and her children are members of the church. Laura Watts is a member of the Deaconess Board and
the Mothers Board, and she is the church clerk in charge of membership
records. She is barely literate, and many church members resent the fact
that she holds that position. Tyrone Watts does not attend church. While
church members agree that Deacon Albert Watts is devoted to the Sunday school program, many do not like the way he embarrasses people
who do not attend Sunday school. Others do not care for his dogmatic
management of the program. Some members resent him also because
he often neglects to pay his tithes and church fees. Watts secures his
position, however, by his dedication to the Sunday School Board.

Deacon Watts's lack of formal education does not hinder his belief
that he has the qualifications, ideas, and motivation to run the Sunday
school. This became clearer one Sunday when my friend Theodore Smith
visited First Corinthians M.B.C to see firsthand how Deacon Watts operated the Sunday school program. At that time Theodore Smith was in
his final year of study in the divinity school at the University of Chicago, and he was completing an internship in a middle-class, ethnically
mixed church on the city's South Side. One of Theodore's assignments
was to revive interest in Bible study among church members, and for
the most part his attempts had been unsuccessful. When I told Theodore
about the large turnout for Sunday morning Bible study at First
Corinthians, he wanted to see how Deacon Watts managed to get the
strong showing. I arranged to have Theodore spend the day with me in
church. The morning he visited, he was warmly welcomed and during
Sunday school was immediately ushered to the front of the sanctuary
near Deacon Watts. Deacon Watts was enthusiastic and filled with pride
with this opportunity to show Theodore how he conducts the program.
After the meal later in the day, Deacon Watts sat with Theodore for a
couple of hours in the fellowship hall to go over Sunday School peda-
gogy and principles to motivate teachers and students to stay with the
program. He made it clear that leading Sunday school is hard work that
requires God-given talent and divine inspiration. He explained that his
ability to discharge his duties is based on his belief that this is what God
wants him to do. Moreover, he stated that leading individuals to regular
Bible study would not be easy because the task of getting people to live
a disciplined life is formidable in a world filled with distractions. He

told Theodore that to succeed, he would have to pray for patience and tolerance.

Though Deacon Watts's hard work is certainly behind the success of the Sunday school program at First Corinthians, it is also true that members attend Sunday school and the other scheduled Bible classes at First Corinthians M.B.C. because they enjoy reading the Bible and discussing the word of God and the power of the Holy Spirit in their lives. In Bible study individuals discuss their personal shortcomings, fears, and doubts. In class they seek spiritual enrichment and affirmation. Bible study for them is essential for developing spiritual strength and knowledge to endure life's hardships. They believe that every human experience is prefigured in the lives of biblical people whose stories provide models for their own lives.

Table 4
SUNDAY MORNING WORSHIP SERVICE

Activity	Performer(s)
Devotion	Deacons in Charge
Scripture	Minister
The Lord's Prayer	Congregation
Musical Selection	Choir
Announcements	Announcing Clerk
"Amazing Grace"	Rev. James Thomas
Sermon	Rev. James Thomas
Invitation	Rev. James Thomas
Benediction	Rev. James Thomas

Sunday Morning Worship Service

As eleven o'clock draws near, the fellowship hall and the corridor leading to the sanctuary are crowded with church members and their guests who have come for the morning worship service (see table 4 for an outline of the service). Approximately three hundred people attend this service, which is one of several conducted at First Corinthians M.B.C. during the week. Through worship services the church seeks to praise and glorify God and to receive spiritual guidance through the Holy Spirit. Members consider church worship a divine gift that prepares human beings to minister to others, as the following statement in Sunday bulletin proclaims: "It is our prayer that through your participation in our worship service you will be blessed and as you leave our worship service to go out into the world you will be a blessing to others.

At 11:00 A.M. two deacons in charge stand behind the offering table at the front of the sanctuary and ring the bell to signal the start of the service. The two men lead the congregation by singing, "When I woke up this morning, I said 'Thank you, Jesus, for this brand new day.'" Members of the Mothers Board, being spiritual leaders, are always among the first to leave the fellowship hall for worship service. As congregants enter the sanctuary, they join in the singing. All worship services at First Corinthians M.B.C. begin with a hymn and devotion. Church members believe that music soothes the soul and opens the heart to receive God's word. Music is used throughout the service to help people receive spiritual insight.

When the sanctuary is half full, one of the deacons in charge rings the bell on the table, signaling the ushers to close all the doors for the devotional prayer, which the two deacons take turns offering. In this audible prayer church officers must make a statement about the problems that burden people through the week. This is the time when congregants must see that, at church, people can take their problems to God and get answers. The devotion must show them that God is listening and capable of acting on behalf of humanity. It always reveals the principle that human beings are united by suffering and loss. In their eyes, only God, who is merciful and compassionate, can rescue humanity from a shattered destiny. Church deacons have different ways of positioning their bodies during the devotion. Some stand and face the ceiling with their hands lifted, others kneel with their backs to the congregation, and others bend over the table or chair with their heads on their folded hands. This is a prayer Deacon Albert Watts offered one Sunday morning, on his knees, with his head and hands on the chair:

> We have our trials and tribulations, and we must thank you, God, for bringing us through it all. Through the heat and the cold and the snow, we are thankful. Somebody don't know you this morning. We ask that you find him. Somebody's heart is broken. We ask that you look on him also. Somebody has called you all night long. We ask that you answer. Somebody is hungry and thirsty. Call on 'em, Lord. We're not calling you because you're hard of hearing or because you're far away but because it is the way we know how to go. We're trying to do your will. I'm standing here and I know I'm not alone. You've been with me for a long, long time. I have watched the

ships go by knowing that you were there. I have been doing what you've told me to do. I've been standing on the threshold of death a long time. I know I'm going to thee. All I ask is enough time to finish the job that you gave me. Lead me down to the cold, chilly graveyard, and I believe you will cross me over to the camp where I will not have to shake the hands I don't want to shake, where I won't be sick no more. Bring me where I won't be mistreated no more; just bring me home. Don't let me come crying. Put a smile on my face. Amen.

The devotion recalls human suffering, death, and hope for everlasting life. It reminds the congregation that God does not fail individuals who have dedicated their lives to him. The purpose of the devotion is to open worshipers' hearts to receive the lessons and inspiration they need from God for their well-being. Members of First Corinthians believe that the heart is hardened by life's difficulties and that a stiff heart cannot receive God.

As they conclude their prayer, the deacons face the congregation and direct the ushers to open the sanctuary doors and seat the latecomers. When everyone is seated, the processional begins. The Gospel Choir and Inspirational Choir march in from the back of the sanctuary and proceed up the side aisles and onto the stage. As the choirs enter the sanctuary, they are preparing the mood of the congregation to receive the word of God. Once the singers are on the stage, they sing a song that they hope will inspire and uplift the spirit of the congregation. It is their job to get the congregation ready for the service and the work of the Holy Spirit. As the song nears the end, Rev. James Thomas walks in from the back of the sanctuary up the right aisle wearing a three-piece suit and carrying a large white Bible with gold letters. The assistant ministers and Deacon B. J. Clark march in behind him. They too are dressed in three-piece suits. Deacon Clark sits with the other deacons in the pews to the left of the pulpit. The ministers take their seats in the semicircle of chairs set up on the stage behind the pulpit. Rev. Thomas sits directly behind the pulpit, surrounded by his assistant ministers and the Gospel and Inspirational choirs. Each of the men who entered the sanctuary with Rev. Thomas will address the congregation during the service.

After the ministers are in place, the congregation stands and recites the Twenty-third Psalm; they are led by Rev. Allen Tyson. The eighteen persons who founded First Corinthians M.B.C. recited this Scripture the night they met in May 1950 to organize the church. Rev. Allen Tyson was present at that meeting. Born in 1901, he is the oldest member of the church and has been a significant spiritual authority at First Corinthians. He is always the first of the assistant ministers to address the congregation. Some mornings, inspired by the Holy Spirit, he preaches for a few minutes before he returns to his seat. As the congregation is seated, an assistant minister—chosen by Rev. Thomas—comes to the pulpit to present the Lord's prayer. The choir stands and softly sings in the background as the minister offers an audible prayer. Rev. Richard Pearson is often chosen to give the Lord's Prayer, which is recited to bring about unity and spiritual empowerment in the church. Rev. Pearson gave the following rendition of this prayer at a service I witnessed at First Corinthians:

Our Father, who art in heaven, hallowed be thy name. Thy kingdom come. Thy will be done on earth as it is in heaven. Give us this day our daily bread, and forgive us our debt, as we forgive our debtors. And lead us not into temptation, but deliver us from evil. For thine is the Kingdom, the power, and the glory.

Lord, we come today as one body, with one mind, with one thought and one spirit. We come today to say, our Father, we know that thou art in heaven today. We know holy is your righteous name. And we ask now, Lord, that thy kingdom come on earth as it is in heaven. We ask you today, Lord, to give us this day our daily bread. Lord, we know that food is good for the body, but you say in your word man should not live by bread alone but by every word that proceeded out of the voice of God. We come, Lord, to ask you to forgive our debt. God, we haven't been right always. We have done people wrong. We ask you also, Lord, to forgive us our debt as we forgive our debtors. Lord, the people who have done us wrong, we ask that you forgive us that we might forgive them. Lord, we ask you lead us not into temptation. Lord, you have the power in the world. You have all power. If you want to lead us into temptation, you could, because you're the power and you do whatever pleases you. But we ask that you not lead us into temptation but deliver us from evil. Lord, we know that evil is in the world today. Temptation is on every side. Lord; the temptation of the world is evil in our life. Deliver us from temptation. For thine is the power. You are all the power, Lord. You are everything in this world. The glory belongs to you. Heaven is yours forever. We just want to behold your glory forever. We know that Jesus Christ is your glory forever. For thine is the kingdom and the power. We know you got the power this morning. We know you got all power in heaven and earth in your hand. We realize that you are God this morning. We realize that no man can come into the garden except if he comes by you. We thank you that you have opened up our eyes and we see now the door of eternity. Lord, the glory belongs to you forever, forever. Now we ask this day be your day. Let us be glad and rejoice because this is the day you made. And you made it, God, that we might glorify your holy name. That we might honor the works that you have done in creation. That we might give you the honor and the praise as Lord and Savior over humanity. Lord, as we come this morning, we thank you that you have been good to us, and we know that we have been bad. And we know that all the bad that come upon us, Lord, it was for our disobedience. And Lord, we thank you that you made a way for us. Lord, we thank you for Jesus Christ this morning. We thank you for the Holy Spirit this morning. We thank you for the word of God. Lord, I thank you for my life today. I thank you for the life that I'm around today. Lord, have mercy this day. Lord, not only have mercy, but we thank you for your mercy today. We thank you for strength that you have given us. We thank you for the power of love that you have given us. We thank you that you didn't give us the spirit of fear but the power and glory of a sound mind. We thank you for this opportunity. And Lord, when this life and this day is over and Lord, we can't retreat nowhere else, we know we have a home that's not made by hand; we know that we have a home in eternity. We know that you are the tabernacle of our new home. Lord, let us come to your kingdom. Lord, let me lay my head upon your back and behold your glory throughout eternity and give you all the glory and the praises. We ask this in your precious son Jesus Christ's name and for his sake. Amen.

The Lord's prayer recalls the unresolved tension between evil and good and the belief that, through Jesus, God has overruled evil. The minister proclaims the universal gift of salvation through faith in Jesus. He lets the congregation know that every human being is capable of violating God, but that God is forgiving and merciful.

After the Lord's prayer the choirs sing before another assistant minister goes to the pulpit to offer the altar prayer. The purpose of the altar prayer is to address crisis, misfortune, and sickness. The minister prays for the afflicted in the church and in the world; he calls the names of church members who are sick at home or in the hospital. Rev. Arthur Johnson is often appointed to offer the altar prayer. The following is one of the prayers I heard him offer:

First is the Lord, the boss man of this great universe. We come as bad children before good things, realizing that we have sinned before your holy will, realizing that we said when we need you, we'll call you. Lord, we need you right now. Realizing that you watched over us last night and bright and early this morning. You taught us with the finger of love. Our eyes flew open.

Everyone can answer that. Realizing that everything was all right when we laid down last night. And when you woke us up this morning, everything was in order. Realizing we know that nobody could have done this but you and you alone. This is why we ask you this morning to hear our prayer. Realizing we're in trouble; our back's against the wall. We tried everything and everything failed. We know that you could give it, God. We know you're a merciful God. Beside thee there is none other. You crossed us from rocking in our cradle up to the present time. Some of us come crippled, Father; some of us come blind. We know you are able this morning. We sure do thank you this morning. You give us water to drink when we're thirsty. Realizing that we don't need water this morning. We need your word this morning. We know your word this morning will soothe our soul.

Please, Sir, have mercy. We sure do thank you this morning. We thank you for another week this morning. You brought us through this morning. We sure do thank you, Father. We thank you for the pastor this morning. Go with him and stand by him. Go with friendship this morning. Friendship needs you, Father. We can't make it this morning. Some folks don't need friendship. We need friendship this morning. We need to come together, my Father. Let us come together. You said, "Let us reason together." We find ourselves by reasoning together this morning. You know every thought this morning. You know the purpose this morning. We have not met together. We have not come together, Father. We thank you for the hearse wagon that didn't knock at our door this morning. You've given us another chance. Please, Sir, have mercy. My Father, go to the sick this morning, all over the land and country. Somebody needs you this morning. Remember Sister Diane this morning. Go with her and stand by her. You brought somebody a long way this morning. Please, Sir, have mercy. Somebody is standing in need this morning. We know you can this morning. Go with Rev. Dixon this morning. You brought him when the doctor had turned his back. We know you're able this morning. We know you're this kind of God this morning. When men have walked away, my Father, they've done all that they can do, that's when you step in. We sure do thank you this morning. You come in our life one day. Men had gave up and could bear no more. That's when you stepped in. We sure do thank you this morning. Go with Father Tyson this morning. There is some who were not here last week. They're here right now, my Father. We know they could not have done this but for the love of you this morning. We know your love this morning, and we sure do thank you this morning. After while, my Father, we need you coming this way. We know you're able. We know we can be saved. Amen.

In the altar prayer the congregation is reminded of humanity's dependence on God for spiritual and physical well-being. The minister enunciates the forms of evil and misfortune in the universe and humanity's inability to overcome them without God's intervention. Sister Diane, whom Rev. Johnson named in the altar prayer, was twenty-six years old and the mother of two small boys. Two weeks before the Sunday Rev. Johnson offered this prayer, three men broke into her West Side apartment, raped her, and severely beat her. She remained in the hospital for four months before she died from the injuries she sustained during the attack. Her mother, Teresa Davis, a member of the church, took care of the boys while their mother was in the hospital and adopted them after her death. She brought the boys to church every Sunday. The church prayed for Diane Davis throughout the four months she lay in the hospital. Her tragically broken body reminded the congregation of the evil that abounds in the universe as a consequence of human beings who are ruled by hate and violence. For church members, Diane's death represented the enigmatic nature of evil and of God's purpose. Her tragedy challenged the congregation's faith and hope in God. In prayers on her behalf in the church and in the ones offered by the Mission Circle groups by her bedside in the hospital, God's healing power and ultimate victory over evil were invoked.

Rev. Johnson also named Rev. Frank Dixon in the altar prayer. Rev. Dixon, as was noted in chapter 3, was one of the church founders and an important church patron in its early years. At First Corinthians M.B.C. he is known as one of the truly saved. In the last years of his life, God was again using Rev. Dixon to demonstrate divine power to overcome affliction. He had colon cancer, underwent several operations, and made it back to church three years beyond the time doctors said he would live. At the end of his life, members of the church referred to him often when they testified about God's healing power. In their vision, only God can reverse disease and dying. At the end of his life Rev. Dixon was self-confident, witty, and kind. His bearing showed the congregation the equanimity and poise God delivers to suffering Christians.

Father Tyson, who was also mentioned in this altar prayer, was at this time enduring the recent loss of his wife, Josephine, who had been his companion for over forty years. He lived alone in a one-bedroom flat. His body was frail, and he was fighting depression. His presence reminded the congregation not to despair in the face of a failing body and social isolation. The altar prayer reveals human suffering and recalls their belief that healing, compassion, and protection come from God.

After the altar prayer, the Gospel Choir and Inspirational Choir sing. The singing is followed by the announcements. Angela Williams is the announcing clerk; Rev. Thomas appointed her to this position in 1984. Diane Cobbs had been the announcing clerk for several years before then; Angela was her assistant. In 1984 Diane Cobbs moved to a suburb. Her husband, who had never joined First Corinthians M.B.C., joined a church near their new home, and she decided to go there with him. The announcements are written by the church secretary, Zena Jackson, and approved by Rev. Thomas on Sunday morning before Angela Williams gets them. Angela is also in the Gospel Choir. When it is time for the announcements, she stands at the microphone to the right of the pulpit facing the congregation. She first presents the Sunday schedule, then announces the programs sponsored by the church groups the coming week and the rest of the month. She names the group and the individuals offering each program and enthusiastically encourages members to attend. "Let us come out and support the program. Come out and get the Word," she might say. "It's a blessing to help others who are working for the Lord." She also thanks those who attended church programs in the past week. Next she recognizes church members who have celebrated a birthday or wedding anniversary during the week and expresses the hope that God will continue to bless them. Finally, she gives the names and phone numbers of church members who are sick and confined. If she has information about their illness, she states it and directs the congregation to pray to God to comfort them and guide their doctors.

Angela Williams is followed by Linda Harris, who makes the travel announcements. Linda Harris is also an officer on the Senior Usher Board. Her husband, T. C. Harris, is a member of Committee Number One. The Harrises have been members of First Corinthians M.B.C. since the mid-1960s. Linda Harris was appointed to this position by Rev. Thomas. She first talks about the trips that took place during the past week; she indicates who sponsored them, where the groups went, and what enjoyable and memorable things occurred. Then she announces the upcoming trips, giving the destinations and the sponsors of the trips, who should be contacted for more information.

Linda Harris turns the congregation over to Rev. Thomas, who has been seated behind the pulpit, hidden away from the view of most of the congregation since he marched into the sanctuary. Every Sunday morning he stands holding the Bible, which he places on the pulpit as he sings "Amazing Grace"; the congregation joins in the singing. Rev. Thomas says he has been singing this song before he delivers the sermon every Sunday morning since he became pastor of First Corinthians M.B.C. because it connects him to God and prepares him to receive God's message. According to him, "Amazing Grace" represents his spiritual transformation from a lost and corrupt man to one who lives to serve God to deliver others from suffering. In Rev. Thomas's mind the song recalls God's power to save humanity. When the song is finished, the congregation settles down for a sermon that will last over an hour and a half.

At the start of the sermon, Rev. Thomas speaks softly and slowly. In his opening remarks he thanks God for bringing them together again to "mingle and commingle our voices." He first reminds the congregation that church fellowship is a blessing. He then presents the topic that will be discussed in the sermon. When he became a minister, he could not read or write; he relies on God's help to develop his message as it is delivered. As he sees it, the purpose of his sermon is to reveal God's blueprint for living. In part, the sermon aims to instruct people on how to live according to God's plan. Rev. Thomas believes his themes are divinely inspired and speaks to the day-to-day circumstances of the congregation. Invariably, at the beginning of the sermon he suggests two or three chapters from the Bible for the congregation to read for what he calls "Bible proof" of the lesson he is about to give. He also assigns a chapter for the following week. Rev. Thomas is considered the church authority on the Bible; it is his job to guide church members as they read and study the Bible.

In every sermon, Thomas illuminates God's plan for the church and for humanity on the one hand and, on the other, reveals the shortcomings of human character that impede the fulfillment of God's vision. He discusses human wrongdoing in the light of God's model. As he brings up the sinful things going on in the world, his voice gets loud, and he pounds his fist on the pulpit to make his point. His manner is severe as he lets the congregation know that he will not overlook their infractions to spare their feelings: "I don't care what you all think about what I'm saying or how I'm saying it because I'm feeling real mean today and the sermon is gonna be real long because there is a lot we need to learn. I'm not afraid of you. All I know is that there is some things going on in this church that is wrong and that God don't like and I'm here to straighten you out." He also lets the church know that he will not take a bribe to soften the message or ignore sin in the church. "Some of you think that, because you bought me a Cadillac, I'm going to stop talking about some things that's wrong in here. Well, you're wrong. God doesn't want me to do that, and I'm not gonna do that. There is some things going on in the church that God wants me to bring up, and I intend to bring them up every Sunday. And if you don't like that, you just take the car back and I'll walk home." While Rev. Thomas discusses sin and indiscretion, his moral authority is ratified by people who nod their heads in agreement. Some confirm his points by shouting such encouragement as "That's all right, preacher," "Say it, preacher," or "Go 'head, Reverend."

The subject of salvation comes up in every sermon. Rev. Thomas tells the congregation that only God can give humanity eternal life. He asks everyone to repent and seek God's mercy. Above all, he stresses that human beings must have faith, mercy, and love in their heart to accept Jesus and to live as good Christians. Having mercy, he explains, means you are capable of feeling and understanding the sorrows that burden others. Love, he says, enables you to be merciful and to help others in their time of need. Faith in God gives you strength to overcome your problems and to help others. However, as Rev. Thomas points out every week, faith, love, and mercy do not come easily to human beings. He says that unless people pray hard and ask the Lord for his help, they are going to think of something and do something that is evil. In his vision, we are born greedy and jealous. As he puts it, "We see the things that other people have, and instead of saying, I hope God keeps blessing you, we get jealous and say, how come I can't have those things?" According to Thomas, humanity is misguided about salvation. As he says, "Men think that if you have money, nice clothes, and fine furniture you're gonna be saved. But I'm here to tell you that all the money in the world won't get you eternal life. The Kennedys is some of the richest folks in the world, and the Kennedys always die. Mrs. Onassis is one of the richest women in the world, and Mr. Onassis died. Mr. Onassis's son died too. So you see, God don't care about how much money you have or don't have. God doesn't need your money."

During the sermon Rev. Thomas also discusses the deep sorrows and conflicts people endure. He speaks of marriages falling apart, husbands who fail to come home at night, children dropping out of school, children using drugs and joining gangs, sickness, violence, insufficient money for basic physical needs, taking abuse from a boss, being mistreated and humiliated at a welfare agency, and the self-contempt that poor blacks develop in a society that treats them with hostility. Rev. Thomas reminds the congregation that life's hardships are part of a divine plan to strengthen people's faith in God's redemptive power. Thus his sermons articulate two parallel themes: how terrible life can get and God's power to deliver human beings from destruction. In the sermon Rev. Thomas always cites examples from the Bible as well as episodes from his own life and the lives of members of his congregation when God intervened to spare them from ruin.

As Rev. Thomas articulates the hardships people face in daily life, he invokes the Holy Ghost. Through his message church members are touched by the Holy Ghost and begin to shout. The Holy Ghost reaches the heart and sets individuals on fire, purging evil from their hearts and restoring love, faith, and mercy. Thomas explains what happens when church members shout in church: "We believe the power of the Word comes from heaven and is given by God. The inspiration of what's been said comes upon us so powerful that we are not able to hold it and therefore we either cry, shout, holler, wave our hands in some form or fashion to let others know that we have had a sign from God that he is pleased and that he is with us." But there are other ways in which people express themselves when they are touched by the Holy Spirit. Some sit quietly with bowed heads, tears rolling down their faces; some sit motionless and say they feel a tingle run through their body. Others stand quietly and move their arms in wide circles. Some kick their feet and scream, "Yes, Lord!" Others feel a rush of heat and shout while they fan their bodies with the palms of their hands to cool off. As individuals shout, members of the Nurse Board and Usher Board protect and comfort them. Anyone who faints is carried to one of the lounges. Children and teens never shout; they stand by and watch. Some of the small children get frightened and cry during the shouting. They are cared for by the nurses or by someone sitting near them.

As the commotion from the shouting fades, Rev. Thomas, who has been leaning over the pulpit, picks up the microphone and walks off the stage from the left singing the invitational hymn, "This Little Light of Mine I'm Gonna Let It Shine." The congregation sings while the deacons arrange the chairs in front of the pulpit for the candidates who will answer the call. After the invitation, Rev. Thomas turns the congregation over to Deacon B. J. Clark, the chairman of the Deacon Board. He is six feet two inches tall and thin. He always dresses in a three-piece suit and carries himself with dignity. He speaks with a firm voice from the microphone on the right side of the pulpit. It is Deacon Clark's responsibility to remind everyone to tithe every week and to pay their other church dues. He acknowledges that while some members pay on time every week, others neglect their tithes week after week; over half the members do not pay their tithes. He lets the congregation know that the comforts they enjoy in church—heat in the winter, air conditioning in the summer, and a place to sit and have a free meal with family and friends—cost money and that everyone must give his or her share.

When Deacon Clark has finished, he turns the church back over to Rev. Thomas, who asks visitors to stand and introduce themselves. Every Sunday morning there are a few people related to or acquainted with members of First Corinthians M.B.C. who come to spend the day. Guests state their names, the names of the people who brought them to First Corinthians M.B.C., the names and locations of the churches they belong to, and their pastors' names. Some visitors also talk about the spiritual benefits they gained from the service. When the visitors have been recognized, Rev. Thomas reminds those who have guests to make sure their company is seated for the meal prepared for the congregation every Sunday in the fellowship hall. He then talks about the programs for the rest of the day and for the week at First Corinthians and asks everyone to support them. Just before he dismisses the congregation, he calls the names of church members who have celebrated a wedding anniversary or a birthday during the week and asks them to stand for a blessing. The congregation stands and sings "Happy Birthday" or "Happy Anniversary" to those who have had a birthday or wedding anniversary. Finally, while the congregation is standing, Rev. Thomas raises his right hand and offers a benediction. The organist and drummer play while the ushers escort people into the fellowship hall. Sunday morning worship service ends between 2:00 and 2:30 P.M. During the last half hour of the service, cooking smells from the kitchen fill the sanctuary.

Church Dinner

In the mid-1970s Rev. Thomas became concerned about senior church members who were not eating adequately. He said that the Lord put it in his heart to have the church sponsor a meal on Sunday so that the seniors would get a decent meal at least once a week. At that time the church program was expanding, and worship services were also held in the afternoon and evening on Sunday. If a meal were provided at church, members could stay there and be ready for the evening services. Before Rev. Thomas established the Sunday dinner, women sold dinners in the fellowship hall; the money they collected went to their church group. The sale of food at First Corinthians M.B.C. has been strictly forbidden since 1976. Rev. Thomas explained that it is a violation of God's will to sell food in church. Food, he believes, should be shared among church members as it is among families. In his view, both church and families become stronger and closer by sharing meals.

In the perspective of members of First Corinthians M.B.C., the free weekly meal sets them apart from other churches, which serve community meals less frequently and charge for them. They are acutely aware of the hunger problem that exists in their midst and in the world. Food shortages and hunger are common themes in Rev. Thomas's sermons and in audible prayers. Most adults in the church have a story about hunger they have endured. Most of the households I spent time in lacked adequate food. The Sunday meal at First Corinthians is a source of solidarity and satisfaction. It is a point of honor with church members to tell people that a free meal is served every Sunday at their church. As they see it, God put it in Rev. Thomas's heart to offer a community meal, and God has blessed them to feed everybody on Sunday. According to Thomas, other ministers send their wives to First Corinthians M.B.C. to see if it is true that a free meal is served to everyone attending the morning service.

Immediately following the Sunday morning worship service, the congregation moves into the fellowship hall for the meal. Rev. Thomas, assistant ministers, and deacons are the first to leave the sanctuary. They form a receiving line near the entrance to the fellowship hall to greet congregants as they enter the room to take their seats for the meal. Rev. Thomas is always at the head of the line. Next to him are his assistant ministers and Deacon B. J. Clark. They are followed by members of the Deacon Board, Committee Number One, Usher Board, and Senior Church Mothers. The room is noisy as congregants rush to find their friends and get a table. Approximately three hundred people participate in the Sunday meal; two hundred can be seated at a time in the fellowship hall.

The Sunday meal is prepared by women from one of the church groups. At the annual church business meeting, which takes place during the last week of November, a "kitchen business" calendar is set up for the year, indicating which group will be in charge of the dinner each Sunday. The group in charge is responsible for planning, cooking, serving, and cleaning. The church provides the food, cooking gas, and facilities for preparing and serving the meal; tithes and funds collected from worship services held in the evening pay for the meal. For the first seven years that the church offered a dinner, Rev. Thomas shopped for the food in the wholesale markets a few miles east of the church. He has since given the job to Rev. Arthur Johnson, who each week buys cases of chicken and large cans of green beans, corn, or peas. If the price is right, he also buys turkey wings and drumsticks, short ribs, or roast beef. Rev. Johnson is also responsible for keeping the church kitchen stocked. Staples in the pantry include cornmeal, cooking oil, sugar, salt, elbow macaroni, pepper, coffee, white flour, American cheese, and cherry-flavored Kool-Aid. Johnson also stocks paper napkins, plates, and cups and plastic cutlery, taking inventory weekly and buying items that are missing or running low.

The women in charge of the dinner plan the meal around the foods Rev. Johnson delivers. They begin this work on Saturday afternoon and resume early Sunday morning; they are not obligated to attend Sunday School or morning worship on the days they cook. Invariably the Sunday dinner includes fried chicken, vegetables, corn bread, and Kool-Aid. On Saturday the women cut and season the chicken; they get nine portions from each chicken. These women may distinguish themselves by bringing dishes from their own homes. When senior women are in charge of the meal, there will be dishes like chitterlings, stewed pig feet and ears, and greens cooked in salt pork, all of which appeal to older members of the church. Younger women prepare spaghetti, macaroni and cheese, macaroni salad, and green salads, which their peers, teens, and children like. Women who are on duty may call their friends and ask them to bring a dish to help round out the meal; women who are not called or on duty may also bring a dish. By offering dishes to the church on Sunday, women gain recognition for their generosity and ability to fulfill the respected female role of providing food. While women prepare and serve food on Sunday, they wear aprons over their church outfits.

Before the food is served, people stand next to their seats while an assistant minister blesses the meal. The women in charge recruit teenage girls and boys to help them serve the food. The pastor's table is always attended first. Seated with Rev. Thomas are the assistant ministers, Deacon Clark, members of the Deacon Board and Committee Number One, and visiting ministers. These men hold the highest status in the church, and their position is evident in their privileged place during the meal. The pastor's table is the only one covered with a tablecloth and set with dishes, glasses, and stainless steel flatware rather than paper and plastic; the tableware has been given to the church over the years. Food for the pastor's table is served on platters that are set on the table. A napkin-lined basket of corn bread and a pitcher of Kool-Aid are also placed on this table. While the men eat, the platters and pitchers are refilled by women in charge of the meal; for them it is an honor to serve the pastor's table. They make sure that what they consider the best portions of the dishes they have prepared are offered to these men. When Rev. Johnson buys short ribs and roast beef, there is never enough to feed even half of the people who stay for the meal. These dishes are offered to the pastor's table first. In addition to the large platter of fried chicken, most kitchen groups prepare roast chicken for the pastor's table.

Rev. James Thomas and the men who eat at his table especially like dishes they ate in the South. Senior church women go out of their way to prepare these dishes to offer the pastor's table. Linda Larson has been cooking for church community meals since the mid-1960s. She and other women show great pride, joy, and determination when it comes to cooking for the church. One Saturday afternoon in August 1984 I went to Linda Larson's daughter's house to celebrate her grandson's birthday. As I parked my car in front of the house, I saw Linda and her daughter, Annie Larson, sitting on lawn chairs out front. Linda looked despondent but perked up when she saw me. She immediately asked me if I would take her to the grocery store to buy food. Annie jumped in and explained that her mother did not need to go shopping for food and had no business cooking. Linda had been released from the hospital earlier that week and ordered to rest at home. Following doctor's orders, Annie refused to take her mother shopping. Linda had been seriously ill, and I believed that Annie was justified in refusing to take Linda shopping. However, Linda explained that she was going to church the next day and that she was going to prepare a dish to take with her. She took her change purse out of her pocket and counted her coins and food stamps while walking to my car and directing me to get in to take her to the store. She had a total of six dollars and fourteen cents. In the car she said that my reward would be a portion of the dish she was about to prepare.

At the store Linda delighted in selecting greens. She also bought salt pork and pig ears and feet. She wanted to buy corn but did not have enough money. On Sunday she triumphantly served her dishes to the pastor's table and to her friends.

The Senior Mothers Board table is next to the pastor's table. Rev. Thomas's wife sits at this table every Sunday with the Senior Mothers. The Senior Mothers do not cook for the church, since their principal obligation to the church is to provide spiritual and moral guidance. Their table is tended after the pastor's table. Except at the pastor's table, a paper napkin, plastic fork and knife, and paper cup are set at each place before the crowd enters the fellowship hall. Individual plates of food are arranged in the kitchen and taken to the tables. The women in charge give what they consider generous and good portions of food on the plates they send to the Senior Mothers. If one of them gets a plate she does not like, she can ask for another one, and her request will be graciously accommodated. Others who are given a plate they are unhappy with know that it would be impolite to send it back. People seated at the same table may exchange plates among themselves. While dishes are distributed, boys and girls serve Kool-Aid from a large plastic container near the kitchen. If a dessert has been prepared, it is displayed on the glass case next to the kitchen at the start of the meal. For dessert there may be a cake and a fruit cobbler. The pastor's table is offered dessert first. There is never enough dessert for everyone who would like some.

Baptist Training Union

The evening program on First Sunday is always well attended. About a hundred people gather in the sanctuary at 4:30 with their Mission Circle Bible group for the Baptist Training Union service. Rev. Thomas is in charge; he selects individuals from different groups to help him lead the class. He and his assistants sit facing the congregation. They lead the group in singing a hymn. A prayer is offered by one of the assistants. After the prayer, Thomas presents a question and asks the groups to discuss it in the light of Scripture. The classes huddle in their seats in the sanctuary, read the Bible, and discuss the question for thirty minutes, after which Rev. Thomas brings the groups together again. He calls on individuals from each class to address the question. Baptist Training Union themes mostly concern the purpose of the church and what God expects people to do in it. Some sessions turn into disputes over church practice.

Baptism Service

On First Sunday the baptism service immediately follows Baptist Training Union. Deacons lift the carpet and boards covering the pool in the sanctuary. Rev. Thomas stands on the stage to the left side of the pulpit over the pool, singing "Remember Me"; assistant ministers and deacons stand by to help him. People gather as the pool is filled with water, and they join in the singing. The candidates, wearing white gowns, white bathing caps, and white socks, sit in the pews on the left side of the pulpit facing the pool. An assistant minister and deacon wearing plastic jumpsuits stand in the pool to immerse the candidates in the water. Deacon B. J. Clark stands near the edge of the pool to help the candidates step into the water.

Church members believe God created baptism to reunite humanity with him after Adam and Eve disobeyed him and fell from grace. Rev. Thomas says, "God created man holy, upright, perfect, and without a blemish. When man ate the fruit that God said he should stay away from, he had sinned and was separated from God." To be saved, a person must confess and have absolute faith and trust in God. Members of First Corinthians M.B.C. believe that the person who is baptized dies into sin upon immersion and is brought up into the newness of Christ upon being lifted out of the water. Baptism does not save an individual, however; it is only the first step, taken to show God that the candidate is a repenting sinner who believes in him and is willing to obey him. To be saved, an individual must endure life's invariable hardships without renouncing faith in God. He or she must seek God through the Holy Spirit in every word and deed and must praise God, glorify God through deeds, and be prepared to go to God with problems. Through the baptism service, Pastor Thomas aims to recreate the feelings surrounding baptism as far back as the day when John baptized Jesus in the river to remind the congregation that Jesus gave them the right to be baptized and to join God in heaven. As the candidates stand in the water, Rev. Thomas also recalls life's difficulties and the divine help that comes through confession and baptism.

The baptism service begins with an assistant minister reading the third chapter of Matthew from the pulpit. After the reading, another assistant minister goes to the pulpit to offer a prayer. As he speaks, the congregation again sings "Remember Me." In one service I witnessed there were six candidates. After Rev. Richard Pearson read the scripture, Rev. Charles Larson offered a prayer:

Our Father, who brought us here again, thank you for allowing us to come for one another. We come this evening to ask you to have mercy. You said you would and you kept your word. Please, Sir, don't leave us this evening because we need you. We can't make it without you. These that's going down in the water this evening decided that they want you to be their ruler, their super ruler over their souls. Go with them and stand by them. Take them by the hand and lead them and guide them. Work it through their heart. We realize Satan is going to get on their track. But you lead them to make Satan leave them alone. Have mercy right now. Go down in the water with them this evening. Come up with them this evening. Go with them and talk with them. Strengthen them where they're weak, and know that they're going to need you more so now than ever before. Have mercy this evening. Be their guide. Be their shepherd. Be their leader and be their strength. In the name of Jesus we pray. Amen.

That evening Rev. Larson's eldest granddaughter, Ladona Evans, who was nine, and his grandniece Lisa Johnson, who was eight, were among the candidates. Rev. Larson's three children and fourteen nieces and nephews have been baptized at First Corinthians M.B.C. After his prayer the congregation sang "Take Me to the Water" while Deacon Clark helped the first candidate step into the pool. The candidate stood between the two men. Rev. James Thomas lifted his right hand over his head and said,

It was Jesus that came to be baptized by John. It was John that stood in the water who had the divine sight of the bank which they stood on. And he said, "Behold the lamb of God, an individual whose shoes I am not worthy to step into." But he said to him, "Jesus suffered for it to be so." But he wanted him to do it for the fulfillment of you and I. Which gives us the right to do it ourselves today, obedient to the great head of the church. According to your faith, my brother, I indeed baptize you in the name of the Father and of the Son and of the Holy Ghost.

The candidate was immersed and raised, then helped out of the water by Deacon Clark as the congregation sang "None but the Righteous." As the second candidate stepped into the water, Rev. Thomas raised his right hand and said,

One thing I am satisfied with, that God does not make any mistakes. While they were standing in the water a dove descended all the way from heaven and landed on Jesus' shoulders. The Bible says he went straight down in the water and baptized and came out and went up into the mountain. When they were at Mt. Transfiguration, Peter said he could hear the same voice that he heard down at the river Jordan where John was baptizing. Therefore I baptize you, my Brother, in the name of the Father and of the Son and of the Holy Ghost.

When it was Lisa Johnson's turn, her father, who had been appointed to stand in the water that evening, raised his right hand over her and said,

I never will forget one warm day. My mind ran back way down in Alabama when they brought me to the creek. Many times I'd been swimming in that water. Many times there were snakes in that water. But I'll tell you, on this particular day I had a feeling that I never had before: the Lord had come to my rescue. And I'll tell you, one day a few months ago, my daughter came to me and told me, "I want to be baptized. . . . I believe that God will save me when I come to die." And she said, "Well, daddy, I know that I will have to keep his commandments to the graveyard." It sure ripped my heart. Obedience to the great head of the church. I baptize you, my daughter. Not because of your confession. Not because of your mother's faith. Not even because of your father's faith. I indeed baptize you because of your faith. Obedience to the great head of the church. I baptize you in the name of the Father and of the Son and of the Holy Ghost.

As the fourth candidate stepped into the water, Rev. Thomas raised his right hand and said,

Obedience to the great head of the church. I tell you, the church has power if you need it. Tell someone I went down in the water through the church's name. Ever since that Wednesday I've trusted the Lord. My faith came one third Sunday evening when they raised their hand, children, and said, "Obedience to the great head of the church." According to your faith, my sister, I indeed baptize you in the name of the Father, in the name of the Son, and in the name of the Holy Ghost.

As the next candidate stepped into the water, Rev. Thomas lifted his right hand and continued:

One of the finest things that ever happened to me. Since I got baptized, I've been broke some. One of the finest things that ever happened to me. Since I got baptized, I've been sick and real low. Since I got baptized, I've been without friends. Since I got baptized, I'll tell you, every time I get in trouble I always call the Lord. One day I went down in the water. Obedient to the great head of the church. My sister, I indeed baptize you. In the name of the Father and of the Son and of the Holy Ghost.

Over the last candidate of that day Rev. Thomas raised his left hand and said,

I'll tell you, every time they baptize I get a feeling not quite as good as that third Sunday. Better than any other feeling I've ever had. Reminds me one day when they was getting ready to take me down in the water. Got an old deacon wading out with a pole in his hand. He kept jabbing the water trying to find how far could he go. I have to tell you that we got way out in the water. After he turned around and looked up towards heaven, I could hear the old preacher when he raised his hand; words came from his mouth saying "Obedience to the great head of the church." According to your faith I baptize you in the name of the Father, the Son, and the Holy Ghost.

Rev. Thomas then offered a closing prayer.

Our Father and our God that gives every good and perfect gift, we just come with thanksgiving in our heart. We come for these that has come today. We thank you, O God, for the home they came from. We pray that it will continue to be a God-fearing home. We do pray now, O Lord, one by one, that you will lead and guide these young people. Throw around them a strong arm of protection. Bless them in a special way. Now Lord, now Lord, I know you know how and I know you know when. I know that you're able to lift up bowed-down heads. We sure do thank you this evening for everything that you have done. Thank you for these young people that went in the water. Bless them one by one. And when they're on their way home tonight, please Lord, go with them and stand by them. Bless them in a special way. Now Lord, now Lord, now Lord, look at the homes they come from. I know you got all power, heaven and earth in your hand. Thank you.

At the close of his prayer, Rev. Thomas led the congregation in singing "Sweet Low, Sweet Chariot." He dismissed the congregation from the baptism service with these remarks:

That sound good, didn't it? Yeah. You can sing that and go all the way back home just singing that song. About a month and half ago I was back in Mississippi. And I thought, let me go down here where my aunt sang that song—the first song I ever heard in my life. I want to go down by this pea field where she used to sing that song. I got down there by that field, and when I got down there I said, My goodness; right along in here is where that old women would sing that song, "Swing Low, Sweet Chariot." And you know we just sit there and talked about it. What a blessing it was. I'm so glad she sang that song that day. I never would have known what it was all about. She just sang that song. Most people think that I be playing—you know, I'm just saying something to make it sound good. But it wasn't. It was a group of almost close to fifty or sixty folks out there, and the peas were dry, and it looked like them vines were saying, "Swing low, sweet chariot." I was just a little young boy; wasn't quite big enough to take a bucket of water. I remember being there. And every time I go down there I stop by that field. I appreciate the fact that that's where I heard my first song at: "Swing low, sweet chariot. Coming to carry me home." See, at that time didn't but a few folks have an automobile. And we got to thinking about that if people who were able had an automobile, then God would have a chariot. Swing low, sweet chariot. All we had sometimes was some fatback to go with the peas. I don't suppose you know what that is?

Through the baptism service church members narrate stories that tie their lives to the legacy of Jesus. They recall Jesus' baptism and the day they were baptized and began to hope that God would guide their lives. At First Corinthians M.B.C. the baptism service is a way the congregation has of placing the circumstances of their collective stories—which include dispossession from land, migration, inadequate wages for labor, and the hardships of living in the ghetto—into the wider context of the Christian story. The congregation seizes a noble spiritual past to reverse the harm that results from their being cut off from land, family, and home in the South and from social and economic opportunity in the ghetto.

The Lord's Supper

On First Sunday, the congregation comes together again at 7:00 P.M. for the Lord's Supper; the sanctuary fills to its capacity for this service. The majority of the people who attend the Lord's Supper have been in church since morning. Just before the service begins, however, other church members, coming from work, dash to the lounges to change from their work clothes into outfits appropriate for church. Members of the Nurses Board, Usher Board, Mothers Board, Office of Assistant Ministers, Youth Angelic Choir, Inspirational Choir, and Gospel Choir are on duty for the Lord's Supper. On First Sunday the ushers and church mothers wear white, and the other members wear their best outfits.

Shortly before 7:00 the deacons, assistant ministers, and church mothers set the Lord's table. The offering table, which ordinarily stands below the pulpit, is put aside. The Lord's Supper table, which is tucked inside when it is not in use, is pulled out and set in front of the pulpit. The Lord's Supper table is considered sacred at First Corinthians M.B.C. Only deacons, ministers, and church mothers can handle it and the items used for the Lord's Supper service. Only the church mothers are allowed to wash, starch, and iron the linen used for the service. These women put a white tablecloth on the table. They set a small basin of water and a white towel on the table, then stainless steel trays, small plastic cups, baskets filled with crackers, and bottles of grape juice. An assistant minister fills the glasses with grape juice and sets them on the trays. He breaks the crackers in the basket. He covers the table with a white sheet and takes his seat behind the pulpit with Rev. Thomas and the other ministers.

At First Corinthians the Lord's Supper is a remembrance of Christ's crucifixion and resurrection. As the church awaits the day of rapture, when they believe Jesus will return to take the saved with him back to heaven, they keep his memory alive by remembering the power of his resurrection. The enactment of the Last Supper brings them back to Calvary and the turmoil Christ endured. For them this service commemorates the last time Jesus ate with his disciples before he was killed in a sinful way. As we have already seen, in this cosmos Jesus' death united humanity and God, who had been separated when Adam and Eve disobeyed God in the Garden of Eden. At First Corinthians M.B.C., Christ is believed to be humanity's only hope for eternal life. Church members believe that this service creates a bond between them and Jesus' suffering. They say, "For one split second the church becomes one with Jesus' suffering on the cross." According to them, the trials and tribulations they have endured during the month are easier to bear when they realize the humiliation and pain Jesus suffered as he died on the cross. Angela Williams said, "The things that God puts on me this month don't seem like nothing when I think of the evil that he let come upon his only Son just to give me a chance to be saved." The service also recalls evil in the world and the protection that comes from church fellowship.

Rev. Thomas stands behind the pulpit and sings a hymn at the start of the service. Officers, choir members, ushers, and nurses immediately take their posts in the sanctuary on hearing the hymn. Congregants are escorted to their seats by the ushers, and most join in the singing. New members who have joined during the previous month are officially recognized as members of the church during this service. They sit at the front of the sanctuary with the Mothers Board. Sister Laura Watts puts a small square white net on top of the head of each new female member. The net is a symbol of the humility these women will show as members of the church. (Males show their humility by joining the church.) When the sanctuary is full, Rev. Thomas signals to the ushers to shut all the doors. A deacon standing near the Lord's Supper table offers a devotion. When he has finished, ushers allow the latecomers into the sanctuary.

At this point Rev. Thomas may include a time for testifying. When the service is running late, however, he skips this and goes to the invitational call. After he addresses candidates who answer the call, he moves behind the Lord's Supper table and offers a fellowship prayer. As he prays, new members go and stand near the pulpit. Then the choir begins to sing "I Know It was Blood," which it will continue to sing throughout the service. Two deacons lift the white sheet covering the table and hold it up while Rev. Thomas, assistant ministers, deacons, and trial deacons wash their hands in the basin. The oldest minister in the group is the first to wash his hands. As they see it, they are washing their hands with the water that poured from Jesus' body on the cross to cleanse humanity. They are doing so to prepare themselves before they offer the Lord's Supper to the church. After the men have washed their hands, they stand next to each other. Rev. Thomas, the first in the line, stands about five feet to the right of the table, facing the congregation. The assistant ministers stand on his left side, and the deacons stand to their left. The deacon standing at the end of the line holds one of the baskets containing the crackers representing Jesus' broken body. On his right, another deacon holds a tray filled with cups of grape juice, representing the blood Jesus shed for the remission of sins. Each person in the congregation comes forward and takes a cracker and a glass of juice. After eating the cracker and drinking the juice, he or she places the empty glass on a tray and shakes hands with the people standing in the line. As congregants move through the line shaking hands, they say "May God bless you."

The ministers are the first to take communion. Then come the deacons, the new members, the church mothers, the congregation, the choirs, the nurses, and finally the ushers. While everyone is standing in the circle and singing the closing hymn, Laura Watts takes off the nets covering the heads of the women who are now officially part of the church. Rev. Thomas always ends the Lord's Supper service with this benediction: "We do not have a Mount of Olives to go to, but we do have our many homes. Let us go there prayerfully. Let the grace of God and the sweet communion of the Holy Spirit rest, rule, and abide with us henceforth, now and forever. Amen."

Weeknight Church Activities

Rev. James Thomas's ambition is to offer church programs every day of the week. His objective is to stem the influence of the secular world in the lives of church members. Since 1965 he has worked with church members to develop church activities throughout the week. There are no activities scheduled at First Corinthians M.B.C. before 6:00 P.M. on weekdays. Monday through Friday, during the day, the church clerk, secretary, and janitor are on duty. Rev. Thomas goes to the office every afternoon to check the mail, return phone calls, pay bills, and work on the church program. Much of his time during the week is spent visiting sick and shut-in members as well as running errands for the church. No activity is scheduled on Monday evening at First Corinthians. Church groups may use the church on that night to hold meetings or rehearse for musical recitals. Group leaders know, however, that most members do not like coming to church on Monday, and they avoid scheduling meetings on that day.

Mission Circle Bible Classes

The Mission Circle Bible classes meet on Tuesdays at 7:00 P.M. Until 1984 these classes were held on Wednesday night after the prayer meeting. The Mission Circle Bible class structure is similar to the Sunday school program. On Tuesday evening church members seek spiritual insight and strength through group Bible study. The Mission Circle is directed by Rev. Thomas. He recruits and trains teachers. He appoints every member to a class according to age, gender, and position in the church organization. More than a hundred people participate in the Tuesday night Bible study program. Rev. Thomas has appointed Rev. Timothy Willis to instruct the forty-five-minute Bible lesson conducted in the sanctuary for all classes. The assembly then breaks up into separate groups for a thirty-five minute lesson. Rev. Willis is the youngest assistant minister at First Corinthians M.B.C. The congregation believes God has blessed him with spiritual knowledge and the ability to teach the Bible. They believe he has a special gift for leading and teaching teenagers in the church. He is assisted by Shepherd Boys who offer a devotional prayer before the Bible study. He also calls on teenage males and females to lead the Bible study discussion. Under Rev. Willis's guidance, teenagers learn to lead the congregation in prayer and Bible study. In this congregation it is believed that teenagers must accept responsibility for the church, so they are given opportunities to exercise spiritual leadership. Tuesday evening Bible study, Sunday school, and the Junior Choir and Youth Angelic Choir give church youth the opportunity for the Bible study necessary for spiritual development. It is by way of these church programs that church youth explore their spiritual gifts and use them for the benefit of the church.

Prayer and Healing Service

Every Wednesday at 7:00 P.M. a prayer and healing service is held in the sanctuary. Church members say that the midweek Bible study and prayer meeting helps them to keep their minds and hearts on God. According to church members, daily life abounds with temptations that distract them from knowing the power of God through the Holy Spirit. Moreover, they believe that the devil strikes in everyday life to make individuals doubt God's power to save humanity from evil and destruction. For church members, the harshness of the ghetto are manifestations of the devil that undermine their belief in God. Through prayer, they can talk to God about their problems, fears, and doubts. They believe that prayer shows their humility before God and their faith in him. In prayer they seek God's mercy and protection against the devil. In this cosmos, God is always ready to listen and answer prayers. As Rev. James Thomas puts it, "He is a prayer-hearing God, and he answers right now." They believe that when God considers prayer, he looks at the individual's heart. The heart of a prayerful person is obedient and humble and full of trust in the Lord. In worship services and Bible classes, church members are encouraged to pray all the time, knowing that whatever the problem, God will listen if the petitioner's heart is right.

During church programs, prayer is often the theme that speakers are asked to address. One Saturday morning in a program sponsored by the Junior Women's Mission group, a member of the Senior Mothers Board, Janet Willis, explained the significance of prayer this way:

> I woke this morning, and I was so tired I couldn't move. Everything ached. My legs hurt bad. Oh, Lord, I could not move my limbs. I knew I had to pray. I knew that if I could just get to Jesus everything would be all right. So I picked up my legs with my hands and lifted myself off the bed. I just crawled to the bathroom. The bathroom is my prayer room in my house. I can shut the door, kneel on that bathroom floor, and really talk to God about some things. And this morning I did that. I put my head down on that floor, and I said, "Jesus, now you know what I need, and you know my pains and my sorrow. And I know that you're a doctor this morning and that you can make it all right." I could feel the Spirit just lift me up. And I got off that floor and started on this brand new day. Thank you, Lord Jesus. So, my sisters, never forget: you can take it to Jesus.

At that program Sister Ora Carson, also a member of the Senior Mothers Board, explained that prayer is the only way to get through the day. She urged the group to call God in prayer to guide their every step.

> God don't care where you are or what you're doing. He just wants you to pray. If you're on the street corner waiting for the bus and you're so cold that you just can't stand it and the bus is nowhere in sight, just pray. If you ain't got the money to take the bus, pray and ask God to strengthen your feet so you can walk on home. When you're walking down them dangerous streets, pray and ask God to walk with you. If you're on your way to the doctor's office, pray and ask doctor Jesus to be there waiting on you. If you got to go to the courthouse to see the judge, pray and ask God to soften the judge's heart. Prayer. Whatever it is, prayer is the answer.

In the eyes of the congregation, human beings are always standing in the need of prayer. For them, prayer is the key to God's love and mercy. Faith and prayer, they say, turn the key to unlock the door to the Kingdom. Members of First Corinthians M.B.C. believe that the devil strikes harder against people who seek Jesus in prayer. As one member explained, "The devil don't like it when you talk to God. He'll try to get your prayer before God gets it." Church members believe that the church must come together for prayer often to strengthen individuals and the group to fight the devil.

For help with daily prayer, church members establish relationships with prayer partners. Rev. James Thomas created the prayer-partner program. Prayer partners visit each other at home and call on the telephone for prayer. They believe that God is pleased when they call up other partners' names before God. Senior church members who are shut-ins especially value telephone calls and prayers from prayer partners. Toward the end of a long prayer Wilma Stevens offered one Wednesday night, she acknowledged her prayer partners:

> Thank you for the prayers this morning. I was down in spirit. And then, Father, when I had them two prayers this morning, I got up like I hadn't been down, Father. You can't do it by yourself. You have got to have somebody to give you encouragement. Thank you for the prayer partners this morning. Thank you for Sister Delaney this morning. Lordy, thank you for Sister Emily Rose. Both of them called me. And I laid there. And when they got through praying, I just clapped my hands and I said "Thank you, Jesus." Wasn't nothing else I could say.

The prayer and healing service is guided by the Holy Spirit. The meeting begins when two or more individuals enter the sanctuary and sing "I'm gonna do what the Spirit say do, do what the spirit say do, do what the Spirit say do. If the Spirit say do, do O Lord, I'm gonna do what the Spirit say do. If the Spirit say pray, pray O Lord, I'm gonna pray if the Spirit say pray." About fifty people participate in this midweek prayer meeting. As individuals enter, they join in the singing and take a seat near the front of the sanctuary. For the prayer meeting, most church members wear casual clothes. None of the church officers are on duty, and no one dresses in uniform. The ministers and deacons wear three-piece suits.

The meeting begins when the Spirit moves one or two people to take charge. They go and stand behind the offering table facing the group. The leader rings the bell on the table and leads the group in another song. After a few minutes of singing, the leader reads Scripture and then prays. As the leader's prayer ends, another person introduces a song that the group sings. Throughout the meeting some will introduce songs while others take turns offering audible prayers. Each person has a particular song that helps connect him or her with the Spirit. It's a song to sing when one feels tired and low and needs help to get through the day. On Wednesday nights church members look forward to sharing their songs with one another.

Church members say that the midweek prayer meeting is a blessing that helps them make it to Sunday. As they see it, every individual must struggle against evil and doubt. On Wednesday night, people praise God, talk to him about their burdens, and seek his help. God, they say "knows about the burdens that come up on you in the week because he put them there." Every human being must confront the test of God-given suffering as Jesus did on the cross. God wants to see if human beings believe in him and will turn to him to step in. By attending prayer meetings, church members believe they are showing God that they are his humble servants and are willing to endure hardship and calamity. According to them, it is important to thank God in prayer for all things. Rosalie Jones, a member of the Senior Mothers Board, demonstrated this in a prayer she offered one Wednesday night:

> Tonight, our Father, our heavenly Father, we thank you for the joy that came this morning. Lord, when I woke up, I opened my eyes and I could see, and that was joy. And then, Father, when I said "Thank you, Jesus," I could hear my own voice, and that was joy. And when I called to all the others in the house, and they answered to their names, that was joy. Joy came in the morning when you touched us with the finger of love and started us out on another new day. And then, Father, when we had bread in the house, that was joy. Then, Father, I looked around, and thank you, for I could creep around as I had been before I laid down. And Father, when I got up this morning I said, "Thank you, Jesus, for this new day." And, O Lord, I thank you for tonight, my Father. All of us that's out here, Father, the devil didn't get us. And thank you for letting all of us arrive in our homes all right. O thank you, Master, O thank you, Jesus, for this blessing tonight. Lord, I would not have been able to make it here but by you being such a good God, O Lord; you let us make it out. O Lord, some wanted to come and wasn't able to make it out. Some could have come, but they just didn't know it. O Lordy, I ask you, God, to go with our church. Bless our pastor wherever he is tonight. Not only him, Father, but all the members that's on the roster tonight. Go with them and stand by them. Go with our assistant pastor tonight. You know he's weak and by the wayside tonight. Go with Rev. Pearson tonight. Hold him and keep him, Father; guide him the right way that you would have him. Not only Rev. Pearson, but Rev. Johnson. He's trying hard. O Lordy, keep his mind stayed on you, Father. Go with the Deacon Board. O strengthen the deacons, Lord. Give them more power and a better understanding. O Lord, go with the Mothers Board. Give them more faith and grace and love. And Lord, I ask you to bless the president of the Mission; O keep her Lord. You know her husband's been sick. Go with him. Touch him. I ask you to touch him tonight. I know you can.

And then, Father, bless our home when we're away tonight. O Master, go with our schoolchildren today and tonight. They was glad when the schools opened up. O take care of them when they're crossing them dangerous streets. You're the only one we can depend on, Lord. Go with the teachers and help them, Jesus, to teach them little ones. Bless this city, Lord. Bless all of us that's trying to get around one by one. Have mercy on us. Have mercy on us, Master. Go in our homes, Father, and run the devil out. O Lordy, just run him out. And when I'm done drinking bitter cups, O Lord, when I can't make step by step no more, O Lord, I got to go somewhere that I haven't been. And Father, you know I don't know nothing about dying. I ask you to come and meet me, Lord.

In prayer, church members acknowledge the fallibility of human beings. In their vision, doctors, civil servants, politicians, teachers, and ministers who are not guided by God will fail. Through participation in the prayer and healing service, individuals seek God's grace, love, and mercy. They believe that their hardships embody a spiritual lesson for them and for others in the church. After they have offered their prayers, participants form a circle and hold hands while Rev. Thomas or an assistant minister offers the healing prayer. This closing prayer is similar to the altar prayer offered every Sunday morning in church. The minister calls up the names of people standing in the circle as well as those who are in the hospital or sick at home. When the meeting has ended, people embrace, shake hands, and thank each other. Church members say they feel great strength, serenity, and solidarity through group prayer.

CHAPTER SIX

Evangelical Religion and Working-Class Black Family Solidarity

The life chances of low-income blacks who live in Chicago's inner city have been cut short by racial discrimination, de facto segregation of neighborhoods and public schools, and severe economic decline. As joblessness among working-class blacks has spread, public hostility heightened and public funds for job training, housing, food, and medical care have been cut back. The withdrawal of public funds for social programs has truncated social institutions and opportunities for working-class blacks and has severely undermined inner-city black families.

Evangelical storefront churches play a major role in framing ideas and principles to help some of these families structure their lives. The family history of Angela and Don Williams, who were married at First Corinthians M.B.C. in their early twenties, provides a good example. Their story shows the disruptive influence of migration, unemployment, and low wages on family life. The concept of family solidarity is privileged in First Corinthians discourse and practice. The Williamses rely on the church organization for concepts and social support to sustain their family solidarity in the midst of a fragile and broken neighborhood. They draw on church cosmology for principles to define a system of personal meaning and identity.

The family history given in this chapter is based on interviews I tape-recorded during my field work. Some of the interviews took place in the home of Angela and Don Williams and others were conducted in my apartment. Angela became one of my key informants in the field, and I spent a great deal of time in her home.

Angela and Don Williams were introduced in the late 1960s by friends who were members of First Corinthians M.B.C. They lived in southwest Austin in 1981, when I first met them. They rented a three-bedroom apartment on the second floor of a two-story red brick building. Their landlord neglected the property. The lawn was always littered and unkept, as was the stairway leading to their apartment. At that time their household included their two children, Nickie and Darrel, and Angela Williams's mother.

Angela Williams was born in West Virginia in 1951. Her parents, John and Lucy Carter, had ten children. The last two died in infancy. Angela is their seventh child. Of her seven remaining siblings, three are sisters and four are brothers. Before Angela's first birthday, John Carter was laid off his job in the coal mines. Unable to find work in West Virginia, he moved to Cleveland, Ohio, where he found a job that enabled him to send money to his family in West Virginia. But he was soon laid off again. This time he moved to look for work in a small town in Michigan, near Detroit, where his parents lived. He soon started working in an auto mechanic shop and sent for his family.

The Carters moved into a converted attic in John's parents' home. Angela dreaded living there. She recalls that her grandparents were mean to her, her mother, and the other kids. Lucy Carter provided her in-laws with groceries and help around the house to please them and persuade them to be less harsh on the children. One thing Angela says she will never forget is that her grandmother would bake corn bread that tasted like cake, but she and her sisters and brothers could get this only by sneaking some, because her grandmother would not give them any.

In Michigan, Lucy Carter attended a Methodist church with her children. Angela and her older siblings were baptized in that church. Angela was seven when she was baptized. For her it was an unforgettable ordeal. The night before the Sunday she was baptized, her mother took her to the home of a church mother who washed Angela's feet and prayed over her. Angela cried and resented the woman and her mother for making her do something she did not understand and feared.

John Carter studied auto mechanics in night school and started his own business in the garage attached to his parents' house. In a few months, however, the garage burned down. Business had not been good before the fire, and Carter decided to move to Chicago. Once again he left his family behind. In Chicago he looked for his friend Sammie Barns, who had left Michigan two years earlier. Sammie Barns helped Carter find work in a gas station. Carter sent money to the family for a few months before he was ready to have them join him. In 1961 the family moved to Chicago and settled in an apartment on the South Side. Although John Carter had steady work, his wages were low; he struggled to support his family. During the first few years, the Carters moved three times on the same block in pursuit of suitable housing.

Throughout her childhood and young adult life, Angela says, "my family did not have anything but a whole lot of love." Her mother prepared meals she could stretch so that everyone in the family would have something to eat—a skill that Angela picked up and uses to make ends meet in her household. Angela said, "Back then when we was growing up, we didn't have what we have now. It was one thing at dinner. My mother never prepared meat and a vegetable and all that. I mean you had a pot of beans and corn bread, baby, and you ate and you went to bed."

Sammie Barns was a deacon at Mt. Zion Missionary Baptist Church, located on the South Side of Chicago. He invited John Carter to join the church. As soon as the Carters settled in Chicago, they started attending services and Bible classes at Mt. Zion, and John Carter also became a deacon. Angela says he was fervent about religion. He insisted that everyone in the family attend church on Sunday. He would not allow cooking or household work on that day. Lucy Carter and the children had to have their clothes ready for church by Saturday night.

Angela's formal Christian education started at Mt. Zion Missionary Baptist Church. The church had a large sanctuary, twelve classrooms in the basement, a kitchen, and a large dining room. In Angela's eyes, the people she met at Mt. Zion M.B.C. were genuine; she believed that they deeply cared about religion and living by God's word. She recalled that they emphasized Christian education and etiquette. Classes were held at church to help members develop a positive attitude toward the church and the community. At Mt. Zion M.B.C. she met people she wanted to be like. She also felt very proud of herself and her family because of the respect they received at church. After three years at Mt. Zion, things took a turn for the worse for the Carters. They left the South Side and moved to the West Side. John Carter was unable to pay the church subscriptions for the family, and they withdrew from the church when they moved. In his new neighborhood, Carter started visiting storefront churches around the corner from their apartment. Angela was fourteen when the family left Mt. Zion M.B.C., and it was a great loss for her. At

Mt. Zion she had had friends, role models, and people who believed in her and respected her.

When the Carter family moved to the West Side, Angela Williams says, "there was no money for anything in my family then." Her parents had nasty fights, and her father stayed away from home. Throughout her childhood, she had viewed her father as someone who could calm any storm. In her eyes he was loyal to his family and, above all, deeply loving. He had high expectations of his children. Angela was bewildered by the change in her father, and her trust in him was shattered in her early teens. She resented his absence from home and her mother's nagging. Within the family Angela was considered smart, capable, and responsible. Her parents burdened her with many of their daily problems. Angela wanted a better life for herself and the family. At fourteen, she perceived herself as grown-up and decided to look for work to help them. She was hired by a woman she had met at Mount Zion M.B.C. who owned a flower shop. Angela was proud of herself because she could handle the job and earn money. She worked all day on Saturdays in the flower shop for ten dollars, of which she gave eight dollars to her mother for household needs and kept two dollars for herself. Her brothers and sisters who worked also paid a household bill every month. Angela's parents allowed her to date when she turned sixteen, and she met Don Williams then.

Don Williams was born in Mississippi in 1949. He was the third of seven children born to Benjamin and Janet Williams. The family lived and worked on what Don Williams said they called a plantation, which belonged to Richard Bridge. From the age of five, Don Williams was in the field working with his family. He picked cotton at the end of the rows. His great-uncle on his mother's side, Papa Arthur, lived and worked with them; Don has vivid memories of Papa Arthur reading the Bible to the family in their home. He said, "One way or another, Papa Arthur would get hold to you when it was time to read the Bible. There was no way to get out of it." Don is not sure if Papa Arthur really could read; he believes his uncle would simply look at the page and talk about Scripture. When Papa Arthur died, Don was deeply impressed by the commotion in the cabin and by all the preachers who came to talk at the funeral.

At First Corinthians M.B.C., when Rev. James Thomas talks about coming up the hard way, Don Williams reflects on his boyhood. One Sunday Rev. Thomas said in his sermon, "All we had sometimes for days was corn meal with water instead of gravy, and sometimes we didn't even get that, neither." Later that day, Don recalled when he and his cousins were hungry and would search along the railroad tracks nearby for spoiled oranges tossed from trains. In Mississippi, Don would go into town with his family every other Saturday in the late afternoon. On Saturday morning, Richard Bridge would let the children pick cotton. They would make from one to two dollars, which they could spend in town later in the day. Before Benjamin Williams bought a used 1949 Chevrolet, the family went into town in a wagon drawn by mules. Don liked to be around his uncle Mac—his father's brother—and the two of them would hitchhike into town since there was no room for them in the wagon. In town, Don said, they would go to the store and buy bologna, crackers, soda pop, and candy. Sometimes they would see a movie.

Don looked forward to visiting his uncle Mac's house, which was two miles from Don's home. He said, "Going into town and visiting my uncle Mac was the only fun we had when we wasn't working. Uncle Mac baked corn bread that taste like cake and roasted peanuts. He was the first in the family to buy a television." When Don finished his chores, he would walk to uncle Mac's house to watch TV and eat. The Williams family went to church once a month. The church was about four miles from their home. For Don Williams, going to church was a chance to get away from the drudgery of the farm and play with other kids. Like most of the children, Don said, he did not pay attention to the church services.

In the mid-1950s there was no work on the farm for the Williams family. Don's uncles had lost their jobs earlier and had left for Chicago. Benjamin Williams decided to move the family to Chicago in 1957. Nine people packed into the car; Don remembers that his brother Curley rode the window the entire way. In Chicago, Benjamin Williams found custodial work at Mount Sinai Hospital. The family settled in a South Side apartment near the stockyards. A year later they moved to another apartment a few miles west of their first one. Don Williams was nine when they came to this neighborhood. Here he met Jesse Larson and his family. Jesse Larson's father, Rev. Charles Larson, was a member of the Heavenly Knights and one of the people who founded First Corinthians M.B.C. Jesse Larson lived next door to Don Williams. Many of Jesse Larson's relatives lived in flats on the same block, and Don soon became part of their social circle. He and Jesse went to school together, played together, and eventually would go to church together.

When the Williams family first settled in that neighborhood, Janet Williams, Don's mother, joined a storefront church near their home. On Wednesday nights a group from church would meet for Bible class in the basement of a member's home. Don said he did not mind going there because they always had refreshments for the kids. Soon, however, he started going to First Corinthians M.B.C. with Jesse Larson. The church was then located in what Don called a raggedy building on Lake Street. It was a small storefront furnished with a few wooden chairs from an abandoned movie theater in the neighborhood. For Don, it was fun to go to church on Sunday with Jesse and his cousins, though the boys were not keen on the religious services. He said, "The preachers preached, but we never paid attention. We always tried to get away and run around the church, court girls, and stuff like that."

Don and his friends did like the music programs, however. They would stand in the back and imitate the singers. The Heavenly Knights inspired the boys the most. The Heavenly Knights rehearsed at night during the week in the Larsons' kitchen. The boys sat on the fence listening to the men sing late into the night until the singers would quit to get to work in time for the night shift. The boys wanted to be like the men in the group. Don, Jesse, and Jesse's cousins started their own gospel group in 1975, shortly after they returned from military service. Deacon B. J. Clark, Jesse Larson's cousin, has been their manager since the group was organized. Everyone in the group calls B. J. Clark "Brother." They look up to him and turn to him for advice. Don Williams was impressed by Clark from the first time they met. In Don's eyes, he had good manners and was respected by everyone at First Corinthians M.B.C. According to Don, he had a steady, good-paying job, drove a nice car, and always wore nice clothes. Clark became a deacon at First Corinthians M.B.C. a few years after the two men met. He was elected chairman of the Deacon Board in 1975 and has held the position since. Don Williams sees in B. J. Clark a family man, a good provider, and one who has kept his family in the church. Don works hard to achieve the same for himself and his family.

When Don Williams was in the eighth grade, he wanted to earn money and be independent. He found a job after school bagging groceries in a South Side store owned by Sam Lieberman. Sam Lieberman liked Don and taught him everything about the business. Throughout high school, Don made enough money at the store to pay for his clothes, school supplies, and bus fare. After he graduated, he continued to work for Sam

Lieberman and went to trade school in the evening. Don worked in Lieberman's store for twenty-two years, during which he was steadily promoted, finally earning a management position. Don is hard-working and capable.

Don and Angela Williams met through B. J. Clark's sister-in-law Thelma Evans. Thelma was part of Don's circle of friends from church. She had met Angela's brother Robert Carter in high school, and they were dating. Don Williams would drive Thelma Evans to Angela's house to meet Robert Carter. One night Thelma phoned Angela to tell her she was bringing some guys over to meet her and her sisters; Don Williams and Jesse Larson were among them. At the time, Angela was dating Jerome Walters, with whom she thought she was deeply in love. Nevertheless, she was immediately attracted to Don Williams. He struck her as cool, quiet, self-assured, and respectable. They went to First Corinthians M.B.C. to hear the Heavenly Knights on their first date. Angela Williams did not like the church at first. She felt people were envious of her because she was a skinny black woman with long hair. She believed that they perceived her as someone who thought she was better than everyone else in the church. When Angela was around, women in the church would flirt with Don, which made her angry and jealous.

Although Angela and Don quarreled often, they were falling in love. He listened to Angela and seemed to understand her problems. She felt that he really cared about her. Angela says, "When I cried, Don cried with me, and I was really impressed by that." He brought Angela flowers, sent her cards, and bought her nice clothes. A few months into the courtship, Angela was pregnant; her son Darrel was born in 1970. Her parents were disappointed and could not accept her having a baby out of marriage. After considerable turmoil, Angela and Don married in 1971 and left for Germany, where he was sent for military service. In Germany, the couple became really close. Angela liked being away from her family and their problems. She also liked staying home to raise her son.

A year and half later Angela and Don were back in Chicago. They rented an apartment in Southeast Austin, renewed their membership in First Corinthians M.B.C., and reestablished their friendship with Jesse Larson and the group. Don went back to work for Sam Lieberman. Angela got a job selling Doctor Scholl's shoes. Before they left for Germany, Angela had been working as a waitress. While Don would have liked for Angela to stay home and take care of the children and the house, they could not manage financially without her income. In 1974 Angela gave birth to Nickie. Angela's company gave her a two-month leave of absence. When it was over, she arranged to pay her mother-in-law to sit with Nickie and went back to work. Angela regrets that she did not stay home to raise her daughter.

Angela and Don have a firm commitment to working hard to support their family and church. According to them, maintaining their family has never been easy, but it became harder when Don lost his job in 1982, the year Sam Lieberman sold his store. Don did not want to collect unemployment compensation and immediately looked for a job. Within a month he was employed in a suburban factory. He found the job through Joseph Evans, who is married to Jesse Larson's sister Jackie Evans. Joseph Evans is a foreman at the factory and has also hired his brother-in-law and two other men who belong to First Corinthians M.B.C. Don Williams had been earning what he considered very good money working for Sam Lieberman; before the store was sold, his annual income was $24,000 plus bonuses, and he had health insurance for his family. At the factory, he was hired for $3.95 per hour with no benefits. According to Don, one good thing about the factory job is the opportunity to work overtime to increase his income. He also drives the church bus on weekends and during the summer to earn extra money.

In the midst of their financial setback in 1983, Angela got pregnant. Though she and Don had not planned to have another child, they were very happy about it. In the second month of the pregnancy, Angela had a miscarriage. This was the beginning of a spiritual crisis for the couple. Before the miscarriage her doctor discovered cysts on her left breast and left ovary. He advised her not to get pregnant again. A few months later Angela returned to the clinic. She was pregnant. The doctor suggested that she consider terminating the pregnancy, but Angela was determined to have the baby. When she became pregnant, she had been working as a sales manager in a women's clothing store, where she earned a good salary and had medical benefits. She held onto her job despite her discomfort from the pregnancy until the company relocated and laid her off. The loss of her job worsened the family's finances. In his second year at the factory, Don was still earning only a fraction of his former income. Although he worked as much overtime there as he could manage and drove the church bus, he barely earned enough to support the family. Angela collected unemployment benefits but lost her health insurance, and they could not afford private health insurance. She left her private doctor and went to Cook County Hospital for prenatal care.

The doctors at Cook County Hospital considered Angela a high-risk case and wanted to see her in the clinic once a week in the second and third trimesters of her pregnancy. For several weeks I accompanied her to the hospital clinic on Wednesday mornings. The discomfort and uncertainty surrounding her pregnancy did not slow her down. She believed that her painful and risky condition was God's way of developing her faith in him and telling her he wanted more from her in the church. While the doctors recommended bed rest, Angela took on more church work. Until she was delivered of her daughter, on a typical Wednesday she would go to the hospital for her prenatal visit early in the morning, then lead a Mission Circle prayer group to visit church members who were confined in the hospital or at home. At that time our Mission Circle stops always included a visit to the home of Rev. Frank Dixon, who was dying from colon cancer, and Diane Davis, a member of the Junior Women, who had been raped and brutally beaten in her home; Diane died in the hospital a few months after the attack. During these visits Angela would comfort people with Bible reading, prayer, and words that assured them of God's power to deliver them from crisis and affliction. After these rounds she would return home late in the afternoon to prepare supper for her family and get everyone ready for the mid-week healing service and Bible study, which together would last more than three hours. Participating in the Wednesday night healing service was an indispensable part of her therapeutic quest. During the service she petitioned God through the Holy Spirit for mercy, courage, and well-being. While at the end of Wednesday I found myself physically and emotionally drained, Angela was full of energy and zeal.

Throughout that period Angela went to church every day except Monday. On Tuesdays she led Junior Women's Bible class; on Thursdays she rehearsed with the Gospel Choir. On Fridays she attended a short Bible study and special worship services. Saturday afternoons she was in the church kitchen to help prepare food for Sunday's meal and supervise children's programs, and on Sundays she stayed in church with her family from 9:00 in the morning until 10:00 at night—and later if there was a funeral. By Sunday night her feet and legs would be severely swollen. While she was fatigued and uncomfortable, she walked away from the church with an air of confidence and a renewed sense of well-being. In her audible prayers and testimony in church she praised God and thanked him for choosing her to do his work. She asked for courage to endure the pain and ambiguity of her pregnancy. She asked God to break down the fears and doubts of the doctors who attended her at Cook County Hospital. Indeed, during her clinic appointments, she did not hesitate to explain to the doctors that God was in charge of her case and they were his instruments. She sought to lighten up the nurses and doctors with prayer and her spirited disposition. After a long and difficult labor, Angela gave birth to the healthy daughter she and Don named Sante Anna but call their "miracle baby." They both believe that God sent Sante Anna to them to intensify their commitment to him and the church. After her birth they found it easier to stay away from drinking and dancing in nightclubs, which had earlier distracted them from their church commitments.

From the time Angela and Don returned from Germany, they have provided stability and support for members of their extended family. In the early 1980s Angela's parents and siblings were having serious personal and financial problems. In 1981 John Carter abruptly divorced Lucy Carter and married another woman. Angela was devastated by her father's actions. Lucy Carter could not support herself and moved in with Don and Angela. Angela's youngest sister, Linda, who was fourteen the year her parents divorced, moved in with their older sister Donna Carter. Lucy Carter found a job working in the kitchen of a public primary school. She also made extra money on the weekends working as a companion to an older disabled woman living in a suburb near the city. Lucy Carter lived with Angela and Don for two years before she rented an apartment, where she now lives with her daughter Linda.

Angela's brother Robert Carter and her three sisters live in Chicago; her two older brothers moved to California. Robert Carter served in Vietnam; Angela says, "He made it back but has never been the same since." He married before he was drafted. His wife left him when he returned from Vietnam. Robert Carter dropped out of high school and has no job skills. He no longer has ties with the friends he had at First Corinthians M.B.C. and will have nothing to do with the church. When he is evicted, hungry, and without money—as he often has been in the last fifteen years—he always shows up at Angela and Don's home. Other members of his family avoid him because they are not in a position to help him.

Angela's oldest sister, Laura Carter, lives in Garfield Park with her two children. She has no job and is on welfare. The children's father, Frank Woods, comes and goes from the household, and the couple have violent fights. According to Angela, he beats Laura and abuses the children. Laura Carter has been in the hospital twice because of Frank's beatings. She and the children have also been evicted from their homes several times and have turned to Angela for shelter and money. Angela has tried to persuade Laura to get Frank out of her life. She also tries to get Laura to join the church, but Laura and her children avoid it.

Donna Carter had two children with Bobbie Gibbs, who would not marry her or support the children; he left and never returned. She supports herself and the children by cooking for a catering company. Since the mid-1980s, business has been slow for the company, and she is often laid off for long stretches of time, during which she collects unemployment benefits. Donna Carter is a strong and independent woman and has managed to provide for herself and her children. Others admire her for raising them without the help of a husband. It hurts Angela to see her sister struggle on her own. She would like to see her marry someone responsible who could help her and the kids and make their life a little easier. In 1984 Don introduced Donna to Marvin Holman, who works with Don at the factory. Angela and Don like Marvin Holman because he goes to church, has a job, and seems to care about Donna. Marvin and Donna have been dating, and Marvin has expressed a wish to marry her, but she is cautious and reluctant to accept his proposal. Angela and Don have been encouraging her to give Marvin a chance.

Angela was also anxious to get Donna and her children back in church. Donna had withdrawn her membership from First Corinthians M.B.C. in the mid-1970s. She was bitter when Bobbie Gibbs abandoned her and the children, and she was uncomfortable as a single parent in a church whose minister scorned out-of-wedlock births and households headed by females. In 1985, Donna believed the Lord was working in her life to bring her and the kids back to church. She rejoined First Corinthians, and the children have been baptized there since. With much encouragement and support from Angela, she and her children have been getting further involved in First Corinthians.

Since the mid-1980s, Angela and Don have made a stronger commitment to their church and have become very serious about learning the word of God and using it to guide them in everyday family affairs. While they have been affiliated with the church since they were dating in the late 1960s, Angela and Don believe that their problems in the early 1980s—the miscarriage, the complicated later pregnancy and delivery, her parents' divorce, her father's sudden death in 1985, the economic and social hardships her siblings endure—are all part of God's plan to get the couple to deepen their faith in God and to save themselves and their family. Angela and Don and their children are in church several times during the week for Bible class, choir rehearsal, prayer meetings, and devotional services. Each member of the Williams family serves on several church groups. Don was a member of Committee Number One from the early 1980s until he was crowned a deacon in 1987. He serves on the Deacon Board, sings with the Heavenly Knights Juniors, and is one of several church bus drivers. Angela teaches the Junior Women's Mission Circle, is a member of the Gospel Choir, and is announcing clerk. Their son Darrel sings in the Junior Choir, is on the Junior Usher Board, and is a member of the third generation Heavenly Knights singers. Nickie is a member of the Junior Choir and the Junior Nurses Board; she is thinking about nursing as a career. Sante Anna stays with the small children in the Sunday preschool and nursery, sings in the children's choir, and spends much of her time in church sitting with her mother or siblings.

At home, prayer and Bible study are part of the family's everyday routine. Don and Angela believe that the only hope they have of protecting their children and providing for them is God. They say, "Only the Lord can hold our children and keep them from getting into drugs, gangs, sex, and all of the other things that's out there for them to get into." At home, Don talks to God daily in prayer. He thanks God for his job, for the overtime he gets at work, for his health, and for the strength to work and provide for his family. Following church doctrine, Don is the spiritual leader of the family and must work to support the family. Angela and other church women who work outside the home consider their jobs secondary to their main roles as mothers and household caretakers. When church women hold jobs, they continue to discharge what they consider to be their God-given tasks of housekeeping, cooking, household shopping, child rearing, and caring for sick family members; they do not expect their husbands to share responsibility for these tasks.

According to Don and Angela, besides the church, their neighborhood has nothing to offer the family. They are fearful and cautious when moving about the West Side. Their children attend public schools. If they could afford tuition, they would prefer to send the children to private schools. The children do not participate in any extracurricular school programs, and they have no friends among their classmates. When Don and Angela are not working and the children are not in school, they stay at home unless they are in church or visiting the homes of church friends or relatives. Their closest friends are other church members who have also made a serious commitment to living according to the tenets and precepts of their church. Don and Angela avoid social relationships with people who do not go to church, and since the mid-1980s, they have stopped going to taverns and nightclubs and avoid alcohol.

Angela and Don and other members of First Corinthians M.B.C. believe that families will not stay together without God. According to them, the devil hates to see a family that is happy and united by love and faith in God. Church families believe that they have to guard themselves against the devil through prayer and Bible study at home and at church. The neighborhood in which Angela and Don live is crime-ridden and impoverished. They and members of their extended family have been victims of street crime. They feel threatened by the violence, despair, and hostility they see in their neighborhood. Church members believe that the church develops in children hope, self-respect, and concern for the rights and welfare of others. In church, children learn discipline and manners. Church is considered the only place where families can find others to help them improve their life chances by developing spiritual qualities.

The Williamses believe that work, shelter, food, health, and friends are God-given. Families that have been blessed must share with others who are in need. God expects families to be obedient and serve him through good work in the church. God wants church families that are well-off to be concerned for relatives and strangers who are disadvantaged. Angela and Don consider themselves blessed and are willing to work for God in any way they are called. While their family budget is restricted, they share their resources to help others; they do not turn anyone away. When they get tired, frustrated, or angry with troubled relatives, they pray to avoid despair and to find the strength to help them. They believe that fatigue, anger, and frustration are created by the devil to stop them from working for God.

Angela and Don, like many other married couples and some single parents in the church, are saving money to buy a house in a decent and safe neighborhood. Parents in the church are dissatisfied with the schools their children attend and would like to move to a neighborhood where the schools are good. Church families also like to have decent clothes, furniture, and automobiles. Material ambitions, however, are tempered by the more important quest for family solidarity, spiritual growth, and salvation. God expects a portion of a family's assets to be given back to him through the church. Excessive material acquisitions on the part of church families at the expense of their obligations to the church are considered a spiritual downfall.

While Angela and Don Williams live in a neighborhood where the signs of economic deprivation abound, they do not view themselves as impoverished and deprived. In their view, troubled human relationships, economic setbacks, and affliction are opportunities for spiritual enrichment and empowerment. They have developed a social identity rooted in the congregation's interpretation of divine charismatic dispensations. These spiritual qualities shape their experiences and give them a way of defining a system of self-worth and purpose to oppose personal despair and ruin. They look to the teachings of the church to help them build lasting relationships among family members and to guide them in daily life as they deal with financial uncertainty, tenuous work opportunities, intractable health problems, random violent crime in their neighborhood, racial discrimination, and inadequate neighborhood institutions and opportunities for social mobility.

CONCLUSION

Black Religious Consciousness and Resistance

This book has been concerned with symbols in the collective thought and practices of the First Corinthians M.B.C. congregation. The interpretation of symbols in this account is based on local exegesis. My analysis has been guided by Durkheim, Weber, and symbolic anthropologists who have worked on religion and the problem of collective meaning and social solidarity. Durkheim's conception of the church as an embodiment of collective sacred beliefs and practices has provided a model for my analysis of conceptions and precepts uniting the members of First Corinthians. Weber's analysis of the charismatic prophet and charismatic religious authority in building religious institutions has guided my analysis of church leadership, vocations, and organizational structure. Following symbolic anthropologists who have worked among oppressed evangelical Christians in the Third World, I have considered the counterhegemonic potential in the congregation's ideas and practices. This book has argued that the interpretation of symbols and meanings framed in storefront churches must take into account the struggle for political and economic power, contested ideas about black humanity, and black contributions to the development of moral and social thought in American society.

Previous sociological and anthropological accounts have failed to provide an indigenous explanation of black evangelical storefront church beliefs and practices. These studies have overlooked the place of evangelical Protestant thought in the black quest for liberation, social justice, and black moral and social solidarity and thus erroneously concluded that black storefront missions are invariably ephemeral and a capitulation to white authority. An adequate account of evangelical storefront churches must include analysis of the historical and social context of which these institutions are a part. The countless storefront churches in Chicago's poor and black neighborhoods collectively constitute a coherent and stable institution for people whose life chances are severely undermined by a declining inner-city manufacturing base, the presence in national political office of conservatives who argue that ghetto conditions are indicative of laziness and immorality created by dependence on welfare, and a public that is reluctant to spend tax dollars on social programs for the poor.

Since the late 1970s Chicago's black inner city has become a harsher place to live. In the same period, storefront churches have flourished in the city. For the most part, storefront churches' positive contributions to the social well-being of poor blacks in the inner city have been overlooked or misunderstood by social scientists and scholars concerned with the black church and with social reform in the black ghetto. With a few exceptions (Marable 1993:255–63; Morris 1984:1–16), scholarly discourse and accounts in the public media in the past decade about what to do with America's black ghettos have disregarded the social ideas and institutions created by working-class blacks who live in them. In a recent account of the black church in the lives of African-American people by Lincoln and Mamiya (1990), scant attention is paid to urban storefront congregations. Although these writers are concerned with the role of the black church in transforming oppressed black inner-city communities (164–273), they do not direct attention to storefront ministries, which, as this book shows, are the embodiment of solidarity and collective action among working-class and poverty-stricken blacks. Despite the growing chasm dividing the black middle class from poverty-stricken blacks, Lincoln and Mamiya (384) would leave it up to middle-class congregations to reach out to reverse the fortunes of the poor. Even Wilson (1987:56–58), who on the one hand posits an economic explanation of ghetto dislocations, argues that the plight of poor inner-city blacks is in part the result of the black middle class's flight from the inner city and increasing isolation of ghetto blacks from middle-class contacts. Lemann (1991:343–53) recommends federal reinvestment in the inner city but is critical of community-based approaches and does not see a role for the ideas, voices, and participation of working-class blacks in determining the development of government-sponsored social programs in low-income black communities.

In my view, the black and white middle class lacks a sense of moral urgency about the poor, and thus it is unlikely that they will be moved to take action to improve their lot. In the American middle class, the concept of individual autonomy is the principal construct for defining personhood (Bellah et al. 1985:142–63). Commitment to social institutions among middle-class Americans is a matter of making personal choices to maximize individual utilitarian goals. Bellah and his collaborators see among the middle class a moral incoherence and an incapacity to articulate a vision of public good. Moreover, members of the middle class whose self-concept is structured by symbols of individual autonomy and achievement have no reason to believe that personal sacrifice and redistribution of resources are necessary elements in social and economic reform programs. For the most part, middle-income Americans believe they have themselves to thank for their success and think the poor are at fault for not taking advantage of opportunities for self-improvement and mobility. Middle-class consciousness does not see a relationship between race discrimination and black poverty. The middle class is also unaware that the comforts the rich enjoy are made possible by exploitation of wage labor where urban blacks are concentrated.

Among scholars and the public the idea that the middle class has an important role in reforming the injustices in American society and the denial of the involvement of low-income blacks in determining their own affairs is supported by the culture-of-poverty thesis (Wilson 1987:13–14). Interpreters who adhere to the culture-of-poverty perspective argue that poor blacks are incapable of mobilizing on their own behalf because they lack moral and social rectitude. This book has challenged that argument with its analysis of church precepts and rigorous labor in a church calling that order the lives of working-class blacks who belong to storefront congregations. The analysis in this book suggests that the storefront congregation is a community-based organization that embodies the capacity to mobilize moral consciousness and inspire public support to create opportunities for inner-city blacks.

Like oppressed Christian communities in the Third World, the members of First Corinthians M.B.C. look to Scripture to redress evildoing. Consciousness and solidarity in the church are framed by the congregation's collective rendering of a sacred cosmos that black evangelical Protestants have been telling and retelling for over three hundred years. For them, God is the creator and ruler over all things in the universe. In their collective view, God is all-powerful and never fails individuals and communities who have faith in his love for humanity. We have seen that this black vision of God as an omnipotent deliverer of oppressed people has inspired blacks to resist slavery, to establish independent churches against formidable odds, and to struggle to transform an unjust society. Church members seek a deeper understanding of their spiritual and moral purpose by pursuing a church vocation. Every person is blessed by the Holy Spirit to work for God and his people. Everyone has a choice between God's way and evil.

The founding of storefront churches is a collective undertaking in which individuals articulate their understanding of their divine gifts through routine collective action. The development of church leadership relies on the gathering of a group that has the capacity to discern charismatic qualities. As chapter 4 demonstrates, Rev. James Thomas depended on the congregation to help him realize what its members believed was his God-given call to lead them, and his ministry was shaped by the ideas and talents of those who surrounded him. Joining a storefront mission is not a casual matter. Once individuals join the organization, they are expected to dedicate a significant part of their time and resources to it. Within the framework of the storefront mission, people build lifelong spiritual careers. Church principles give labor, money, and the things money can buy moral and social value. Labor and the fruits of labor are God-given for his purpose, and a portion of the harvest must be returned to him through church stewardship. In this cosmos the privileges of economic advantage are subverted by the certainty of death and the hope for eternal life through faith in God, who conquered death.

In the storefront church, low-income blacks create ways of thinking about the world and acting in the world that reverse degrading public assumptions about inner-city blacks and the privileged position of individual self-interest in mainstream American thought and life. In contrast to people who demonstrate middle-class unencumbered individualism, members of First Corinthians M.B.C. look to Scripture in group Bible study for exemplary stories and people to help them shape their personal identities. Church members defer to the authority of the church for spiritual guidelines that will inform their deportment in everyday life. In their collective discourse, the well-being of the community depends on personal sacrifice and generosity. To their way of thinking, greed and selfishness may be the keys to accumulating wealth, but they inevitably create social isolation and personal confusion. In the moral and social teachings of this congregation, personal achievements and material accumulation are of value only when they are used for uplifting the group.

The cosmos for members of First Corinthians M.B.C. is ordered by their collective understanding of Jesus' life, his teaching, and his death and resurrection. Through the collective routines of the church they seek to learn moral and social principles by which to interpret their experiences and relationships with others. In Jesus' story they see the spiritual gifts of patience, love, prophetic wisdom, and humility used to dismantle worldly oppressors and evildoers. Their hope is to emulate the principled life that he led. However, the fulfillment of their moral and social vision based on their biblical narratives and precepts is truncated by a political economy that exploits the working class and despises poor blacks. The congregation's ideas and hopes for improved social and economic opportunities are up against a market-oriented economy driven by a thirst for profit at the expense of meeting basic human needs for affordable housing, a decent education, access to health care, and a wage that is above a mere subsistence level. In the congregation's thinking, as this account shows, greed, indifference, and exploitation are the evils church members must combat if they are to claim their fair share of America's abundant resources.

The storefront congregation is an agency within the black ghetto that launches an ideological attack against the evils of racism, greed, and economic exploitation by positing a worldview that defies the hegemonic ideas of the rich and powerful. The thinking of political and economic elites that minimize black worth and potential are challenged by the church's views about equal human value before the eyes of God and divine authority over material resources. Racist stereotypes about lazy, ineffective, immoral, and unresourceful blacks are contradicted by rigorous church protocols, steadfast commitment to work for the church, and creativity and skill on the part of the community of believers to maintain the storefront mission. In church discourse and practice, members meaningfully address the problems they have securing work; the violence and crime they endure in their neighborhoods; the deprivation they see on the ghetto streets; and the hostility, indifference, and humiliation they suffer because they are poor and black. In the consciousness of the church, the onus for the ruined black inner city is placed on the greed and corruption of the dominant group. In church the congregation reaches for beauty, dignity, fairness, self-affirmation, and satisfaction to withstand poverty, exploitation, injustice, and suffering. Members of First Corinthians M.B.C. do not see themselves as an impoverished and marginal community. In their cosmology there is a meaningful vision of black suffering, hope, and self-determination. In church discourse and practice, members liberate themselves from demeaning social ignorance, prejudice, and scorn. In their narration of the Christian story they seek to reveal spiritual truths that affirm human equality and the coming of the day when social justice will prevail.

AFTERWORD

James Thomas died on May 14, 1993. The last time I saw him was in mid-February 1993, when I was back in the field with a team from a local firm seeking to develop job opportunities for unskilled workers on the West Side. I had set the meeting up with Deacon B. J. Clark, who also chaired the church Finance Committee, and I did not expect to see Rev. Thomas that evening. We were very glad to see each other, and he immediately started to tell me about the new church building they had acquired. Just that week they had purchased an abandoned Catholic church in the neighborhood. Rev. Thomas's enthusiasm was based mostly on the fact that the building included facilities for a school: one of his dreams was to see the congregation run a Christian primary school. At last, he believed, that was within reach. First Corinthians sold the old building to another black congregation, abandoned the architectural plans for the new building for which many had committed funds, and moved into the former Catholic edifice in April.

Angela Williams called me early in the morning to let me know that Rev. Thomas had died and that the funeral would be held in the new church building on Sunday afternoon. The new church was located less than two miles from the former site. Automobiles were double-parked near the church, and I ended up finding a space a few blocks away. I walked past several abandoned buildings with broken windows and crumbling walls; they were cluttered with debris. I received hesitant glances from people I encountered on my way. These were unfamiliar and perilous streets. I approached the church steps and saw many faces I knew well as I was greeted by Deacon Clark, Deacon Don Williams, and Deacon Albert Watts. I also exchanged greetings with some of the original members of the Heavenly Knights. The steps leading into the church were jammed with people, as was the hallway leading to the sanctuary; all of the seats were filled. I stood in line and gradually made my way to the front to salute Rev. Thomas one last time. Near the front I saw his widow, two daughters, and grandchildren. They were surrounded by relatives who had traveled from Mississippi for the funeral. I also saw Angela Williams sitting with her daughters and some of my other friends from the Mission Circle. On all of these faces I saw deep sorrow and estrangement. Initially I did not know how to interpret their demeanor. I felt somewhat disoriented. In the storefront that they had created and that I had come to know, I could recognize spiritual vocations, status, and meanings encoded in uniforms, seating arrangements, and worship protocols. I could not readily put my friends into perspective in this vast room with its towering dome, a frieze depicting Christ's passion, stained-glass windows portraying church saints, and dramatic statues of the Virgin Mary and Christ.

I walked up the side aisle and stood in the back to follow the service that would soon begin. In just a few minutes Angela Williams's daughter Nickie came to escort me to a seat next to her mother. As I worked my way to the front, I felt self-conscious about taking a seat when so many had to stand. Angela, wearing a white suit and white hat, sat quietly crying. We had not seen each other since my wedding in September 1992. With a sadness in her voice that I had rarely heard, she whispered, "I'm lost in here. This place is just not right for the First Corinthians M.B.C congregation. We can't feel the Spirit in here, and it's a shame that Pastor's funeral has to be like this." During the service that afternoon, Angela kept repeating that she could not feel the presence of the Holy Spirit.

Rev. Frank Dixon, Rev. Allen Tyson, and Rev. Charles Larson had all died since the mid-1980s, and I had attended their funerals at First Corinthians M.B.C. I recall that on those occasions the congregation rejoiced, knowing that these saved individuals were on their way to rejoin God the Father in heaven. In the vast sanctuary designed for Roman Catholic masses, away from the familiar setting of the storefront that they had converted and fashioned to meet their spiritual purposes, they were unable to attain solidarity, solace, and a sense of confidence about the future of the congregation. Unlike the other funerals of church founders, Rev. Thomas's did not create an atmosphere of jubilation. His sudden death, the loss of the old building that had served as a refuge and home for the congregation for nearly thirty years, the economic burden of the new building, and a succession struggle among the ministers that began to unfold that afternoon created a mood of despair and uncertainty among Rev. Thomas's followers.

A few months after the funeral, Angela called me to tell me that I had to get back with the church to get the rest of the story. Her voice had regained its characteristic optimism and enthusiasm. She told me that the church had spilt. Her family, the Larsons, and a few other families were now holding church services in the basement of Rev. Arthur Johnson's home. She said, "Fran, you have to see this to believe it. The Lord is really doing some truly amazing things. When we get together on Sunday it's like our old church again. You can just feel Pastor Thomas's power. Rev. Dixon, Rev. Larson, Rev. Tyson, and all of our church founders are right there with us. It's like they're not dead. They are right there in church with us and moving us to praise and worship God. There is a job for everyone who comes, and right now we need everyone to work for the church. The children and the grandchildren of the church's founders are keeping it going. You should see Rev. Charles Larson's grandchildren praise God and sing on Sunday. My daughter Sante Anna is leading the Junior Choir. Deacon Don Williams is teaching Sunday School. Anne Larson is leading the Gospel Choir, and her husband is the superintendent of the Sunday school. We've set up a pulpit and loudspeakers. We have about thirty people in the choir. We're trying to buy a building, and right now we're looking at a Hispanic Baptist church that is just beautiful and has everything in it we need. It has classrooms, a nursery with twelve beds, a beautiful wood pulpit. They want a lot for the building, but we are praying that we can work it out with them soon because it's getting real crowded in the basement on Sunday."

When Rev. Thomas died, it was not clear who would succeed him. This led to conflict and eventual schism. Some members of the congregation believed that, among the church's assistant ministers, Rev. Arthur Johnson should lead since he was the one Rev. Thomas had relied on in recent years to assist him in conducting church worship and administrative tasks. Another group, however, insisted on appointing someone who was formally educated. Rev. Johnson is in his mid-forties and lacks formal seminary training. His preparation for the office and his ordination had taken place in the First Corinthians M.B.C. congregation. Deacon Leroy Smith, who led the charge to bring in an educated minister, claimed that Rev. Thomas had told him that in the event of his death, Smith was to make certain that no one from the Larson family be elected to the pastor's office. Rev. Johnson is married to Charles Larson's niece and thus had another strike against him.

Deacon Smith and his faction prevailed. They brought in Rev. John Holmes, who is in his mid-forties and is a formally educated minister. As soon as Rev. Holmes took over, he started to remove members and close friends of the Larson family—this included Angela and Don Williams—from their leadership positions in the church and to give these positions to members who supported him. After a short period of chaos and pain under Rev. Holmes's leadership, about sixty members left the group to start anew under the leadership of Rev. Johnson. Angela explained that, while it was very hurtful to lose First Corinthians M.B.C. to strangers after she and the others had invested twenty-five to thirty-five years of service and support in building it, they could rejoice in knowing that they were free to worship again in a manner that made sense to them. She said, "Freedom to worship is where I get my strength." She declared that the Holy Spirit was once again in charge of the group, and the group's mission was to spread the word of God and thus give others a chance to seize their God-given gifts to serve the church in order to rescue humanity.

REFERENCES

Ahlstrom, Sydney E. 1972. *A Religious History of the American People*. New Haven: Yale University Press.

Ammerman, Nancy T. 1987. *Bible Believers: Fundamentalists in the Modern World*. New Brunswick, N.J.: Rutgers University Press.

Anderson, Alan B., and George Pickering. 1986. *Confronting the Color Line: The Broken Promise of the Civil Rights Movement in Chicago*. Athens: University of Georgia Press.

Anderson, Elijah. 1978. *A Place on the Corner*. Chicago: University of Chicago Press.

Anderson, Benedict. 1983. *Imagined Communities: Reflections on the Origin and Spread of Nationalism*. London: Verso.

Asad, Talal. 1973. *Anthropology and the Colonial Encounter*. London: Ithaca Press.

Aschenbrenner, Joyce. 1975. *Lifelines: Black Families in Chicago*. New York: Holt, Rinehart and Winston.

Baer, Hans A. 1984. *The Black Spiritual Movement: A Religious Response to Racism*. Knoxville: University of Tennessee Press.

Baer, Hans A., and Merrill Singer. 1992. *African-American Religion in the Twentieth Century*. Knoxville: University of Tennessee Press.

Banton, Michael. 1966. *Anthropological Approaches to the Study of Religion*. London: Tavistock.

Bellah, Robert el al. 1985. *Habits of the Heart: Individualism and Commitment in American Life*. Berkeley: University of California Press.

Billingsley, Andrew. 1968. *Black Families in White America*. Englewood Cliffs, N. J.: Prentice-Hall.

Bourdieu, Pierre. 1979. *Outline of a Theory of Practice*. Cambridge: Cambridge University Press.

Boylan, Anne E. 1988. *Sunday School: The Formation of an American Institution*. New Haven: Yale University Press.

Chicago Fact Book Consortium. 1984. *Local Community Fact Book: Chicago Metropolitan Area*. Chicago: Chicago Review Press.

City of Chicago, Department of Planning. 1983. *Chicago Statistical Abstract, Community Fact Book, 1980 Census*.

City of Chicago, Department of Planning. 1984. *Report of the Mayor's Task Force on Hunger*.

Clark, Kenneth. 1965. *Dark Ghetto: Dilemmas of Social Power*. New York: Harper and Row.

Comaroff, Jean. 1985. *Body of Power, Spirit of Resistance: The Culture and History of South African People*. Chicago: University of Chicago Press.

Comaroff, Jean, and John L. Comaroff. 1991. *Of Revelation and Revolution: Christianity, Colonialism, and Consciousness in South Africa*. Chicago: University of Chicago Press.

Cone, James H. 1975. *God of the Oppressed*. New York: Seabury Press.

———. 1984. *For My People: Black Theology and the Black Church*. New York: Orbis.

Daniel, Vattel E. 1940. *Ritual in Chicago's South Side Churches for Negroes*. Unpublished Dissertation, University of Chicago.

———. 1942. "Ritual Stratification in Chicago Negro Churches." *American Sociological Review*. Pp. 352–61.

Davis, Allison. 1941. *Deep South*. Chicago: University of Chicago Press.

Douglass, Frederick. 1963. *Narrative of the Life of Frederick Douglass, an American Slave*. New York: Dolphin.

Drake, St. Clair. 1940. *Churches and Voluntary Association in the Chicago Negro Churches*. W.P.A. Project Official Report 465–54–3–386.

Drake, St. Clair, and Horace Cayton. 1945. *Black Metropolis*. New York: Harcourt, Brace.

Du Bois, W. E. B. 1903. *The Negro Church: A Social Study*. Atlanta: Atlanta University Press.

———. 1911. *The Souls of Black People*. Chicago: A. C. McClurg Co.

Durkheim, Emile. 1965. *The Elementary Forms of Religious Life*. New York: Free Press.

Durkheim, Emile, and Marcel Mauss. 1963. *Primitive Classification*. Chicago: University of Chicago Press.

Eddy, Norman. 1958. "Storefront Church Religion." *Religion in Life* 27:68–85.

Evans-Pritchard, E. E. 1956. *Nuer Religion*. New York: Oxford University Press.

Fauset, Arthur H. 1971. *Black Gods of the Metropolis*. Philadelphia: University of Pennsylvania Press.

Fernandez, James. 1982. *Bwiti: An Ethnography of the Religious Imagination in Africa*. Princeton: Princeton University Press.

Franklin, Frazier. 1932. *The Negro Family in Chicago*. Chicago: University of Chicago Press.

———. 1949. *The Negro in the United States*. New York: Macmillan.

———. 1974. *The Negro Church in America*. Chicago: University of Chicago Press.

Franklin, John Hope. 1974. *Reconstruction after the Civil War.* Chicago: University of Chicago Press

Gans, Herbert. 1962. *The Urban Villagers.* Glencoe, Ill.: Free Press.

Geertz, Clifford. 1968. "Religion as a Cultural System." In *Anthropological Approaches to the Study of Religion,* edited by Michael Banton. London: Tavistock.

Genovese, Eugene. 1974. *Roll, Jordan, Roll: The World the Slaves Made.* New York: Vintage.

Gutman, Herbert. 1976. *The Black Family in Slavery and Freedom 1750–1925.* New York: Pantheon.

Hamilton, Charles Larson. 1972. *The Black Preacher in America.* New York: William Morrow.

Hannerz, Ulf. 1969. *Soulside: Inquiries into Ghetto Culture.* New York: Columbia University Press.

Harrison, Ira. 1966. "The Storefront Church as a Revitalization Movement." *Review of Religious Research.* Pp. 160–63.

Hauser, Philip, and Evelyn Kitagawa. 1953. *Local Community Fact Book.* Chicago: Chicago Community Inventory, University of Chicago.

Health Systems Plan for the City of Chicago. 1984. Chicago Health Systems Agency.

Hicks, Beecher H. 1977. *Images of the Black Preacher: The Man Nobody Knows.* Valley Forge, Penn.: Judson Press.

Hippler, A. E. 1974. *Hunters Point: A Black Ghetto.* New York: Basic.

Hopewell, James F. 1987. *Congregation: Stories and Structures.* Philadelphia: Fortress.

Hunter, James D. 1983. *American Evangelicalism: Conservative Religion and the Quandary of Modernity.* New Brunswick, N.J.: Rutgers University Press.

Johnson, Joseph A. 1971. *The Soul of the Black Preacher.* Philadelphia: Pilgrim Press.

Johnston, Ruby. 1956. *The Religion of Negro Protestants.* New York: Philosophical Library.

Katznelson, Ira. 1973. *Black Men, White Cities.* Chicago: University of Chicago Press.

Keil, Charles. 1966. *Urban Blues.* Chicago: University of Chicago Press.

Kornblum, William. 1974. *Blue Collar Community.* Chicago: University of Chicago Press.

Lancaster, Roger N. 1988. *Thanks to God and the Revolution: Popular Religion and Class Consciousness in the New Nicaragua.* New York: Columbia University Press.

Lemann, Nicholas. 1991. *The Promised Land: The Great Black Migration and How It Changed America.* New York: Vintage.

Levine, Lawrence. 1977. *Black Culture and Black Consciousness.* Oxford: Oxford University Press.

Lewis, Hylan. 1955. *Blackways of Kent*. Chapel Hill: University of North Carolina Press.

Liebow, Elliot. 1967. *Tally's Corner*. Boston: Little, Brown.

Lincoln, Eric. 1974. *The Black Experience in Religion*. New York: Anchor.

———. 1984. *Race, Religion, and the Continuing American Dilemma*. New York: Hill and Wang.

Lincoln, Eric, and Lawrence H. Mamiya. 1990. *The Black Church in the African American Experience*. Durham: Duke University Press.

Love, Emanuel King. 1888. *History of the First African Baptist Church*. Savannah: Morning News Print.

Lynch, Hollis. 1973. *The Urban Black Condition: A Documentary History, 1866–1971*. New York: Thomas Y. Crowell.

Marable, Manning. 1983. *How Capitalism Underdeveloped Black America*. Boston: South End Press.

———. 1991. *Race, Reform, and Rebellion: The Second Reconstruction in Black America, 1945–1990*. Jackson: University Press of Mississippi.

Marsden, George, ed. 1984. *Evangelicalism and Modern America*. Grand Rapids, Mich.: Eerdmans.

Marsden, George. 1980. *Fundamentalism and American Culture: The Shaping of Twentieth Century Evangelicalism 1870–1975*. New York: Oxford University Press.

Marty, Martin. 1970. *The Righteous Empire: The Protestant Experience in America*. New York: Harper and Row.

Mathews, Donald. 1977. *Religion in the Old South*. Chicago: University of Chicago Press.

Mauss, Marcel. 1967. *The Gift*. New York: Norton.

Mayor's Office of Employment and Training. *1979–1982 Chicago Monthly Labor Force Data, City of Chicago Department of Planning*.

Mays, Benjamin, and Joseph W. Nicholson. 1969. *The Negro's Church*. New York: Russell and Russell.

McLoughlin, William G. 1978. *Revivals, Awakenings and Reforms: An Essay on Religion and Social Change in America, 1607–1977*. Chicago: University of Chicago Press.

Meier, August, and Elliot Rudwick. 1968. *From Plantation to Ghetto: An Interpretative History of American Negroes*. New York: Hill and Wang.

Moore, Sidney H. 1975. *Family and Social Networks in an Urban Storefront Church*. Unpublished Dissertation, American University.

Morris, Aldon D. 1984. *The Origins of the Civil Rights Movement: Black Communities Organizing for Change*. New York: Free Press.

Mukenge, Ida R. 1983. *The Black Church in America: A Case in Political Economy*. New York: University Press of America.

Myrdal, Gunnar. 1944. *An American Dilemma: The Negro Problem and Modern Democracy*. New York: Harper & Brothers.

Neitz, Mary Jo. 1987. *Charisma and Community: A Study of Religious Commitment within Charismatic Renewal*. New Brunswick, N.J.: Transaction Books.

Nelsen, Hart, and Anne Kusener Nelson. 1975. *Black Churches in the Sixties*. Lexington: University of Kentucky Press.

Nelsen, Hart, Raytha L. Yokley, and Anne K. Nelsen. 1971. *The Black Church in America*. New York: Basic.

Ogbu, John. 1974. *The Next Generation: An Ethnography of Education in an Urban Neighborhood*. New York: Academic Press.

Paris, Arthur. 1982. *Black Pentecostalism: Southern Religion in an Urban World*. Amherst: University of Massachusetts Press.

Paris, Peter. 1985. *The Social Teachings of the Black Churches*. Philadelphia: Fortress Press.

Parsons, Talcott, and Kenneth Clark. 1966. *The American Negro*. New York: Houghton Mifflin.

Public Service Report Series Number Two, Selected 1980 Census. 1983. Chicago: University of Illinois.

Raboteau, Albert. 1978. *Slave Religion*. New York: Oxford University Press.

Rainwater, Lee. 1967. *Behind Ghetto Walls: Black Families in a Federal Slum*. Chicago: Aldine.

Reid, Ira de A. 1926. "Let Us Prey." *Opportunity*. Pp. 274–78.

Rose, Dan. 1987. *Black American Street Life: South Philadelphia, 1969–1971*. Philadelphia: University of Pennsylvania Press.

Sahlins, Marshall. 1976. *Culture and Practical Reason*. Chicago: University of Chicago Press.

Schnieder, David, and Raymond Smith. 1978. *Class Differences in American Kinship*. Ann Arbor: University of Michigan Press.

Sernett, Milton. 1975. *Black Religion and American Evangelicalism: White Protestants, Plantation Missions, and the Flowering of Negro Christianity, 1787–1865*. Metuchen, N.J.: Scarecrow.

Sernett, Milton C. 1985. *Afro-American Religious History: A Documentary History*. Durham: Duke University Press.

Shimkin, Demitri B., Edith M. Shimkin, and Dennis A. Frate. 1978. *The Extended Family in Black Societies*. The Hague: Mouton.

Simms, James M. 1907. *The First Colored Baptist Church in America*. Philadelphia: J. B. Lippincott.

Simpson, George. 1978. *Black Religion in the New World*. New York: Columbia University Press.

Simpson, Robert B. 1970. *A Black Church: Ecstasy in a World of Trouble*. Dissertation, Washington University.

Smith, Wallace C. 1985. *The Church in the Life of the Black Family*. Valley Forge, Penn.: Judson Press.

Spear, Allen. 1967. *The Making of a Negro Ghetto 1890–1920*. Chicago: University of Chicago Press.

Stack, Carol. 1974. *All Our Kin.* New York: Harper and Row.

Sutherland, Robert. 1928. "Analysis of Negro Churches." Ph.D. dissertation: University of Chicago.

Suttles, Gerald. 1970. *The Social Order of the Slum: Ethnicity and Territory in the Inner City.* Chicago: University of Chicago Press.

Sweet, Leonard I., ed. 1984. *The Evangelical Tradition in America.* Georgia: Macon University Press.

Turner, Victor. 1982. *The Forest of Symbols: Aspects of Ndembu Ritual.* Ithaca, N.Y.: Cornell University Press.

Valentine, Betty. 1978. *Hustling and Other Hard Work: Life Styles in the Ghetto.* New York: Free Press.

Warner, R. Stephen. 1988. *New Wine in Old Wineskins: Evangelicals and Liberals in a Small-Town Church.* Berkeley: University of California Press.

Washington, Joseph. 1972. *Black Sects and Cults.* New York: Doubleday.

———. 1964. *Black Religion: The Negro and Christianity in the United States.* Boston: Beacon.

Weber, Max. 1978. *Economy and Society.* Berkeley: University of California Press.

West, Cornel. 1982. *Prophesy Deliverance: An Afro-American Revolutionary Christianity.* Philadelphia: Westminster Press.

Whitten, N. E., and J. F. Szwed. 1970. *Afro-American Anthropology: Contemporary Perspectives.* New York: Free Press.

Whyte, William F. 1960. *Street Corner Society.* Chicago: University of Chicago Press.

Williams, Melvin. 1974. *Community in a Black Pentecostal Church.* Pittsburgh: University of Pittsburgh Press.

Wilmore, Gayraud. 1983. *Black Religion and Black Radicalism: An Interpretation of the Religious History of Afro-American People.* New York: Orbis.

Wilson, William. 1978. *The Declining Significance of Race.* Chicago: University of Chicago Press.

———. 1987. *The Truly Disadvantaged: The Inner City, the Underclass, and Public Policy.* Chicago: University of Chicago Press.

Woodson, Carter. 1921. *The History of the Negro Church.* Washington, D.C.: Associated Publishers.

INDEX